MAKING YOUR PARTNERSHIP WORK

DANIEL RICKETT

PARTNERS
International

WINEPRESS **WP** PUBLISHING

Packaged by WinePress Publishing, PO Box 428, Enumclaw, WA 98022. The views expressed or implied in this work do not necessarily reflect those of WinePress Publishing. The author is ultimately responsible for the design, content, and editorial accuracy of this work.

Unless otherwise noted all Scriptures are taken from the Holy Bible, New International Version, Copyright © 1973, 1978, 1984 by the International Bible Society. Used by permission of Zondervan Publishing House. The "NIV" and "New International Version" trademarks are registered in the United States Patent and Trademark Office by International Bible Society.

ISBN 1-57921-419-3
Library of Congress Catalog Card Number: 2001095621

Dedication

*To my mother, Luella Rickett,
whose life exemplifies what it means to
"look not only to your own interests,
but also to the interests of others."*

Acknowledgments

A book like this, though written in one year, is the condensation of many years of trial and error. My gratitude goes to the early leaders of Partners International, such as Allen and Ruth Finley, Al and Lorry Lutz, Fred and Dorothy Simmonds, all of whom demonstrated how to serve others responsibly, help without hurting, and receive as well as give. I am especially grateful for the way they encouraged me to learn and channeled my passion by lending their wisdom.

I am grateful to Paul-Gordon Chandler, president of Partners International, for endorsing the project and cheering me on. As the work developed, Phil Arendt, Samuel Chiang, and Bob Savage provided vital input. Chuck Bennett and Kay Marshall Strom made valuable improvements to the early manuscript. Thanks to Steven Downey for handling the many details of the publishing process.

Finally, special thanks to the many leaders and coworkers of partner ministries who embraced me like a brother and welcomed me into their lives and ministries.

I offer this book with gratitude to those from whom I have learned and hope that partnerships in the gospel will become the leading strategy of 21st century missions.

Content

Foreword

Every once in a while, an idea is born ahead of its time. In 1943, four businessmen and an Irish missionary met in a living room in Seattle where they agreed that if China was to be reached with the Gospel, the work had to be done by Chinese Christians. The idea was remarkable for its time: that indigenous believers could be entrusted with the resources to do God's work!

Partners International—founded in that Seattle living room—tested that idea in the crucible of "doing mission" in all parts of the world, and is grateful to God that churches have grown and been strengthened on both sides of the partnership.

Today the idea is seen as the way things *must* be. I doubt those men in 1943 imagined that "partnership" would become the prevailing wisdom of today's missions movement, but experience has shown that *true* partnership in the gospel is used by God to bear fruit for His Kingdom.

God has given Partners International six decades of "lessons learned," and this book is our offering back to Him and His Church. Instead of each church and mission organization (in whatever nation) learning by themselves the lessons of partnership, this book provides the principles and practical tools for engaging in the kind of partnership among God's people that will be a blessing to the nations.

Rev. Paul-Gordon Chandler
President/CEO, Partners International

Preface

This book is for missionaries and anyone else who would say, "I am with you in the ministry of the gospel."

"I am with you" are the four most solemn words spoken in a relationship. "I am with you" is reminiscent of Jesus' promise of authority. It echoes the promise of covenant and evokes the hope of fellowship.

That longing began to come alive in me twenty-nine years ago. I've been working at partnering in the gospel ever since. My travels have taken me to over three dozen countries on five continents. Without exception, in every place I have met extraordinary men and women of God.

But before I had been anywhere, I met a Christian man from India. My wife and I were visiting a tiny church in a tiny town in northern Michigan. The man told of his ministry in India, the orphans he cared for, the school for Christian workers, and the churches he had planted. He was a small man, not particularly impressive, except that he seemed to be as spiritually rich as he was materially poor.

I forgot about the man from India until months later when we received a letter. He explained about his son's desire to go to Bible College and asked for help. We were just beginning to learn to do whatever Jesus asked, and we knew he said, "Love one another." It only seemed fair that if we could go to Bible College our brother in Christ ought to have the same opportunity.

Two years later we had managed to gather enough money to bring the young man to the United States and enroll him in college. Unfortunately our intentions were pure but our plan was flawed. The young man was not prepared for Bible College. It was his father's wish and not his own. He returned home within two years and without completing his studies.

It was a crushing disappointment. We had sacrificed a great deal and did our best to act in brotherly love, but it all came apart and everyone got hurt.

While all this was happening, God was growing in us a passion to love, honor, and serve his people in the hard places of the world. We were expecting our first child and as we were looking forward to his birth, we were also asking God to bring our vision to life. God had other plans. Our son died shortly after birth.

As only God can do, he used the failure, disappointment, and loss to galvanize our sense of purpose. Like a seed that must fall into the ground and die, the death of our son was the birth of a lifelong calling to serve the servants of God in the hard places.

As happens with many young people, our passion exceeded our knowledge. Our view of how to serve our brother from India was simplistic. We had no idea of the cultural issues involved and it never crossed our minds that he could get a better education in India.

It wasn't until we joined Partners International (then Christian Nationals), that we discovered how little we knew. The collective wisdom of the mission saved us from making all kinds of mistakes. By that time Partners had been "assisting nationals" for over thirty-five years. They had learned a lot of things the hard way and did a lot of things right. We had the unique privilege of learning from both.

The purpose of this book is to capture some of that collective wisdom and present it in a way that others can use it.

As I present ways to build and manage ministry partnerships, I recognize that no book is a foolproof guide to successful
partnerships. Partnership is not a technology that can be engi-
neered if you have all the right parts. Principles and practices
that may be gleaned from experience, as I have done here, can
be very helpful, but they are no substitute for the careful and
prayerful reflection on the Word of God for divine guidance.
Seeking to build a partnership without a firm grasp of the nature and calling of the community of God can result in separat-
ing Christians rather than uniting them. With that disclaimer I
feel comfortable sharing what I have found to be the central
shared aspects of effective ministry partnerships.

What Every Partnership Needs to Succeed

Richard Makuyane grew up knowing nothing of the gospel of Jesus Christ. He was born into a poor family in a poverty-stricken village in South Africa. As a young man he fled to Pretoria in search of work. There he fell into a culture of crime and alcohol, and it eventually landed him in prison. But God had other plans for Richard.

In time Richard found forgiveness for his sins and assurance of salvation through Jesus Christ. The first thing he did was to share his newfound faith with others. He began preaching on a street corner to the long lines of people who were waiting for the bus. After the fourth day, the bus driver said to the last man in line, "Pull that man into the bus so he can testify in here!"

When the crowds grew too large to preach on the bus and street corners, Richard borrowed a tent and continued preaching. Often 1,500 people gathered under the tent to hear him proclaim the riches of God's grace. Richard's only desire was to serve God, and God blessed his faithfulness. What began with one man has grown to encompass more than 10,000 new brothers and sisters in the Lord. To date, Richard has seen 16 churches planted in South Africa, Mozambique, Zambia, and Zimbabwe.

For the first time in history, stories like Richard's can be found on every continent and nearly every country of the world.

It is hardly news that the global expansion of Christianity is causing massive changes in world evangelization. Three-fourths of all Christians today live in Africa, Asia, Latin America, and Oceania. As Gordon Aeschliman observed, "From a purely statistical point of view, Christianity is a non-Western religion."[1]

Today a local presence of the Body of Christ can be found in each of the 189 countries that comprise the United Nations. More significantly, a sustained Christian presence (including "underground" churches) exists among 94 percent of the world's people.[2] Thus, as Andrew Walls has noted, the "center of gravity," of global Christianity has shifted from north to south and from west to east.[3]

This is not merely a shift in numbers of people, but also a shift in associated outreach and ministry. In a study of non-Western missions, Larry Pate found that the movement was growing at a rate five times faster than Western missions.[4] Pate projected the number of non-Western missionaries would exceed 164,000 by the turn of the century. And these are only the missionaries who can be counted. There are also innumerable local pastors, evangelists, and Bible teachers, as well as countless lay ministers in countries such as China.

Charles Van Engen, Professor of Mission at Fuller Theological Seminary, sums it up this way:

> In spite of the obvious needs facing the church, Christians around the world today speak more languages, possess greater resources, have the Bible available in more languages, have greater facility of travel and communication, have more qualified leaders, have a deeper awareness of the cultural imprisonment of the gospel, and possess a deeper sensitivity to the cultural issues in mission than at any time in the church's history.[5]

The shift in the center of gravity of Christian expansion is the defining trend of world evangelization today. Not only is it reshaping the grand, macro-level aspects of missions but the local aspects as well, including where, when, how, and with whom Christians carry out the work of the gospel. At every level—personal, local church, denomination, and international mission—the new era of missions is opening worlds of opportunity, making brotherhood and partnership possible at a scope never before realized in the history of Christianity.

The Growing Need for Collaboration

The dramatically changing landscape of world evangelization is forcing new alliances in missions. In the past, since there were relatively few local ministries, missionaries could advance the gospel simply by showing up. Over the past three decades, however, advances by so-called Two-Thirds world churches and missions have altered the landscape. In the face of extraordinary success by local ministries and increasing challenges to the traditional methods of sending North Americans, many missions have begun to recognize the missing links in their ministry capacity and to seek allies in the global neighborhood of Christians.

Simultaneously, international travel and communications have become more accessible to North Americans, allowing them to bypass traditional missions and engage directly in overseas ministries either through their local church or independently. This forces missions to accommodate direct involvement or lose donors to hands-on ministries. It also creates new demands for collaboration.

In the old pattern of missions, the rule was: Make your plans, send your people, and you will make progress. Send more people and you will make more progress. There were only a few exceptions to this pattern, such as emigrant missionaries and those who supported indigenous missions.

In the past few decades the old pattern has been broken. Today you can find communities of Christian witness nearly everywhere. And they are growing. Few places remain where North Americans should pioneer a ministry without at least conferring with local Christians and others who are also active in the area.

I certainly am not suggesting that world evangelization is coming to a close or that there is no place for North American missionaries. On the contrary, the task has never been larger or the cost greater than it is today. More than four billion people still do not know Jesus Christ as Savior and Lord. Most of them live in nations where Christians are harassed, imprisoned, or even executed because of their faith.[6] Yet in spite of the cost, local Christians are sharing the love of Christ and planting churches with astonishing success, very often in places out of reach to conventional missionary methods. Their courage and sacrifice calls for our partnership, but not necessarily our technology, our methodology, or our wealth. What it calls for, and what Two-Thirds world Christians ask for, is our personal, passionate involvement as coworkers in the ministry of the gospel.

In this new world, the rule will be: Build alliances, coordinate your strategies, and you will make progress. Focus more on working together and you will make more progress. We have come to that historical moment when, if we are to be for the gospel of Christ, we must also be for each other.

The world is changing in ways that make partnerships virtually essential to world evangelization. Partnerships are simply a better way to do missions.

Types of Cooperative Structures

Partnership is an old idea with many variations—everything from marriage to internationally networked organizations. So, what kind of partnership does this book envision?

Most commonly, partnership is defined in terms of how people and organizations connect. With the advances in information technology, strategic alliances, networked organizations, and even virtual corporations have redefined traditional ideas about partnership. In this book the focus is not on networked alliances but on the deeper relationships of one-to-one partnering.

It is also defined in terms of who is doing the partnering. In recent years missions consultations have focused on partnership with churches, with donors, with North American missions, and with Two-Thirds world missions.[7] Obviously, who you are (individual, church, or mission) and where you are from (Africa, Asia, Europe, Latin America, North America, or Oceania) has a major bearing on the dynamics of the partnership. Although the emphasis here is on relationships between North American and Two-Thirds world missions, the principles apply to all types of bilateral partnerships.

Individual ministries find many ways to leverage their strengths and opportunities by collaborating with other ministries. These vary from loose associations to tight mergers. Figure 0.1 illustrates an alliance continuum, in which the vertical axis is a measure of involvement, ranging from casual association up to highly integrated participation. The horizontal axis is a measure of interdependence, ranging from modest transactions to permanent relationships.

An association is the affiliation of independent ministries with a common interest in mutual encouragement and a limited exchange of resources. Associations represent the widest range of contacts and the smallest sphere of cooperation between

Figure 0.1. Alliance Continuum

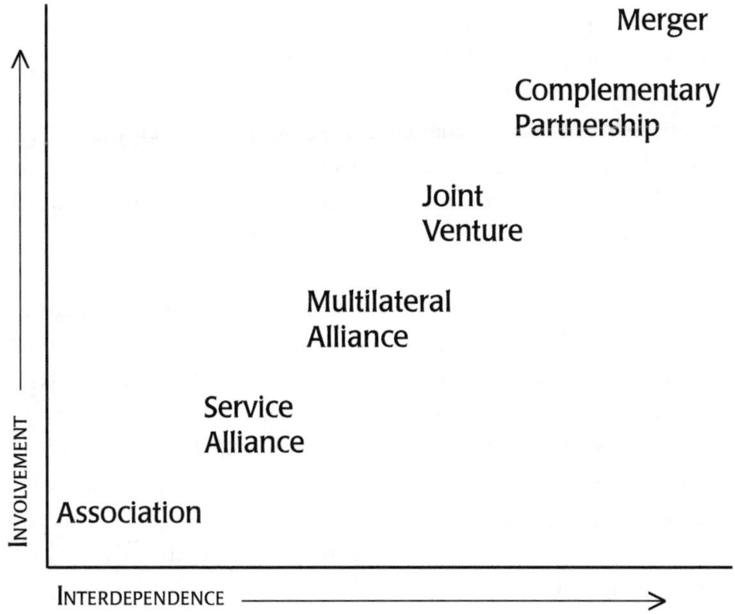

participating organizations. Examples include Advancing Churches in Missions Commitment (ACMC), Christian Community Development Association (CCDA), Evangelical Fellowship of Mission Agencies (EFMA), National Association of Evangelicals (NAE), and World Evangelical Alliance (WEA), formerly World Evangelical Fellowship (WEF).

A service alliance is an association of independent organizations in which one supplies resources or services to the other. Service alliances are transactional in nature; focus is on the funds to be provided or the services rendered rather than on building a relationship and sharing a destiny. Foundations, for example, have a vital role in funding ministry programs, but they rarely have intimate partnerships with grant recipients. Similarly, a wide variety of specialized organizations—such as shipping companies, travel agents, and technology specialists—provide better service by keeping a narrow focus.

A multilateral alliance is an association of independent ministries that correlate separate action toward a common purpose. The multilateral alliance resembles the "vertically integrated alliance" as defined by Phill Butler—an alignment toward a single, overall objective of specialized ministries, such as Scripture translation, medical work, broadcasting, economic development, and evangelism.[8] Multilateral alliances involve several organizations, including specialized ministries and churches, and may work in a broad geographical region or specific community.

A joint venture is the short-term alliance of independent ministries for a limited or specified purpose. For instance, if you develop a series of water wells in cooperation with another ministry, that is a joint venture. Joint ventures rarely involve more than two or three organizations and are often spawned within multilateral alliances. Small-scale development projects are common examples of joint ventures—primary health care, nutrition education, water purification, agriculture, reforestation, veterinary services, and so on.

A complementary partnership is a long-term alliance of two or more organizations that share complementary gifts and abilities to achieve a common purpose. In this book, partnership is defined as a relationship between ministries and people who share common aspirations, strive to achieve them together, and do so in a spirit of cooperation and brotherly love. By this definition, partnership involves making the partner an extension of your own ministry.

A merger is the incorporation of one ministry into another whereby personnel, finances, and programs are integrated into one organization. One example is the 1995 merger of Worldteam and Regions Beyond Missionary Union to form World Team.

In this book the focus is on the more highly integrated, interdependent relationships of joint ventures and complementary partnerships.

The Imperatives of Partnership

What does it take to partner effectively in ministry? What can ministry leaders do to create the relationships needed to share the love of Christ in today's increasingly hostile environments? To have productive partnerships, we must have vision, relationship, and results. No one of these can be ignored. Reduce a partnership to a vision only, and it becomes no more than good intentions. Reduce it to relationship, and it becomes fellowship without a purpose. Reduce it to results, and it loses its capacity to remain faithful. Vision, relationship, and results depend on one another for wholeness. They are interwoven in partnership and in ministry at its best.

By *vision* I mean a compelling view of the future—a picture of what the partnership can achieve. By *relationship* I mean the way partners feel toward one another—genuine expressions of respect, concern, and trust. By *results* I mean the things partners get done together—the outcomes of joint effort.

Taken together the three dimensions provide an overview of the simplest and most fundamental ideas of partnership. Taken

Figure 0.2. The Imperatives of Partnership

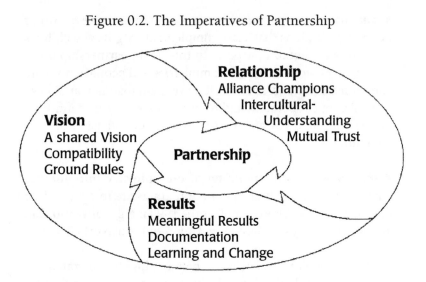

separately each one adds depth and detail to different aspects of partnering. In all there are nine parts to the whole picture of partnership, three within each dimension, as shown in Figure 0.2.

Building a partnership with this model is somewhat like using a zoom lens on a camera. Vision, relationship, and results are wide angle views. Each allows you to see the major parts of partnering, but the detail isn't visible. Zooming in on one dimension allows you to see more about each of the major subparts. For example, the close-up view of vision sees shared vision, compatibility, and ground rules. After having considered those subparts and their interrelationships, you can then zoom back to the wide angle to review the other parts of the entire picture.

Whether you look at partnership through the three wide angle views or the nine close-up views, each is essential to the effective design and management of a partnership. Think of it as the parts of the human body: at times some parts require more attention than others, but a lack of attention to any part could prove harmful or even fatal to the whole.

One way to clarify the various parts of partnership and how they interact is illustrated in Figure 0.3. By asking the key questions of a partnership as if it were currently underway, the interplay of each imperative becomes more evident.

Figure 0.3. The Imperatives of Partnership Design

	Imperative	Key Question
VISION	Shared Vision	What has God invited us to do together?
	Compatibility	What binds us together? What could tear us apart?
	Ground Rules	How do we work together?
RELATIONSHIP	Alliance Champions	Who is responsible to make it work?
	Intercultural Understanding	What cultural differences may help or hinder the relationship?
	Mutual Trust	What gives us confidence in each other?
RESULTS	Meaningful Results	What difference will it really make in the work of the gospel?
	Documentation	How do we keep track of agreements, contributions, and outcomes?
	Learning and Change	How do we handle changes, opportunities, and disappointments?

Each imperative is linked to all the others. For example, the vision you share depends in large part on the degree of your shared values and priorities. How you achieve your vision depends in part on how you work together. Creating a climate of trust and understanding depends on the skill and commitment of alliance champions. Achieving the results you promised reinforces trust. Getting the right results, however, depends on the clarity of the vision and the ability to learn and adjust as circumstances and expectations change.

When these imperatives are mutually understood and internally consistent with the aims and priorities of each partner, they can produce a surprisingly strong partnership.

This book is about partnering—but at a deeper level it is about brotherhood and sisterhood in Christ. Brotherhood in the global neighborhood is a relationship of Christians from different cultures and walks of life who seek to honor their oneness by bearing one another's burdens and joining together in the work of the gospel. Such brotherhood is practiced in its highest form in intercultural partnerships.

Part One: Vision

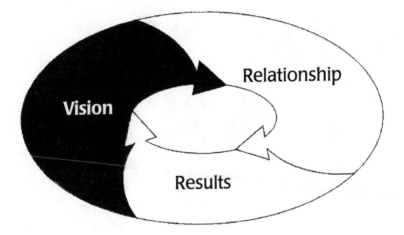

1

A Shared Vision

Shared vision is to partnership what the North Pole is to the compass. It exerts a certain gravity that tends to align everyone's actions with the partnership's avowed purpose and values. Vision is important to any type of ministry, but it is essential for intercultural partnerships. Conventional organizations hold together for a variety of reasons. Sometimes people band together because the outside environment is harsh. Sometimes past successes create a surplus of loyalty that the ministry can run on long after it has run out of vision.

Global partnerships, however, can easily lose their way. Their loyalties are divided because their external threats and opportunities are different, as are their internal strengths and weaknesses. This pushes partners in separate directions. Global partners need a center of gravity. The partners must know why they are partnering and know they are all working toward the same overall objective. Shared vision keeps everyone moving in the same direction.

What is Shared Vision?

Shared vision is a picture of what a partnership can achieve. It establishes both clarity of purpose ("Why we are doing this?") and clarity of direction ("How we are going to do it?"). By vision I mean a picture of the future that is both compelling and credible. A compelling vision is a vivid image of how the future will be different from the present in some important ways. The more richly detailed and visual the image, the more easily the partnership is oriented around it. A shared vision also has to be credible. A credible vision articulates a realistic view of the future. People on both sides have to believe that with God's help they can actually make the vision a reality. But shared vision is more than a mere picture of the future.

A shared vision is also more than a point on the horizon. It is the guidance system of a partnership. Like a ship's rudder, shared vision is what enables you to steer the partnership toward desired results. This is accomplished when partners spell out the underlying purpose of the partnership, establish a clear sense of what the partnership can accomplish, and clarify how each party will benefit from the endeavor.

The Evangelical Theological Seminary of Indonesia (ETSI) is an excellent example of the power of shared vision. In the late 1970s a seminary student from Indonesia had a dream. A single American mission had the foresight and courage to invest in that dream.

Chris Marantika dreamed of an Indonesian seminary that would plant churches. Allen Finley, then CEO of Partners International, believed that if he treated Chris with dignity and supported him as one ordained by God, the investment would be good for Chris, for Indonesia, and for the work of the gospel. And he was right.

Since then, nearly 117,000 Indonesians have professed Christ. Over 1,200 new churches have been started. Today there are 16 mini-seminaries with over 1,000 students, 5 graduate programs with 400-plus students, and another 1,400 students in liberal arts schools. What began as one man's vision is today a world renowned church planting seminary.

Through partnership, the power of the vision reached far beyond Indonesia. Not only were Chris Marantika and his colleagues empowered to build their dream, countless individuals and churches in America have enjoyed the blessings of vital involvement in the work of God in Indonesia.

A Good Reason to Partner

The first element of successful partnership is having a good reason to partner. That seems obvious but it isn't always so. Partnerships start for a variety of reasons, and they are not always good ones. That is to say, the reasons aren't always good *enough*. For example, "to help someone" is not a good enough reason to partner. Why not? Because it assumes a one-sided view of partnering. In fact, it is not partnering at all. It's helping. It's fine to be helpful and to provide assistance, but that doesn't make a partnership. Partnership must be reciprocal. Each partner has something to give and something to receive.

Partners International wanted to share the love of Christ in Indonesia but they were committed to doing so only in alliance with Indonesian Christians. Chris Marantika had a unique vision for the work of the gospel in Indonesia but he needed the resources, contacts, and moral support of an established ministry.

Partnership starts with a recognized need for collaboration. This is the first step in framing a shared vision. It all starts when an organization recognizes a need it cannot satisfy without some type of cooperative relationship. Unless an organization has recognized a gap in its own ministry capacity, it doesn't have a good reason to partner.

So what is a good reason to partner? One that has at least these three qualities:

- It sheds light on why the organizations need each other.

- It reveals what can only be gained through partnership.

- It answers the question, "Why partner?"

Yet having a good reason to partner is only the beginning. It's like the seedbed for growing more specific ideas of what the partnership can accomplish. Once you have a good reason to partner, discussions can move forward toward specific goals and expectations.

What the Partnership Can Accomplish

Shared vision is the result of finding out what God is inviting you to do together. No one ever stumbles across shared vision or drifts into collaborative relationships. It requires yielding to God and to one another by means of the Spirit's leading. And that takes time and deliberate attention.

Typically, the vision of what needs to get done comes a long time before it becomes clear *how* to get it done. Figuring out how to translate vision into reality takes a repeated and conscious effort to sharpen the focus. The surest way to focus vision is by establishing goals that make a difference.

Before going further, a definition of goals is in order. Missionaries and ministry leaders use a number of terms to describe an end toward which activity is directed—and not always with consistency. I use the term *goals* throughout this book to refer to those essential outcomes that make the partnership worthwhile. Whatever partners want to have or become at some point in the future are their goals. Whatever you call them—aims, goals, objectives, or intended outcomes—everyone involved in the partnership needs to know the potential results that will move the partnership closer to its purpose and vision.

Goals are necessary but they don't have to be overly precise. A goal should be stated broadly enough to allow flexibility and clearly enough so that you can recognize it when it happens. If in the course of time the goal doesn't make sense, revise it or throw it out. A goal should never be allowed to become a straightjacket. It is meant to be the point of reference of a shared expectation. If your expectations change, change the goal.

But not just any goals are sufficient; they must be goals that make a difference. In any partnership there are a few critical goals that will provide the greatest contribution toward achieving the vision. Such goals have the following qualities:

- They bring real value to the ministry of the gospel.

- They align the strategic interests of the partners.

- They take full advantage of the skills, resources, and talents of each partner.

Goals that make a difference reflect a potential for impact in the ministry of the gospel that could not be achieved without the partnership. Other goals may be considered, but if they don't add up to this standard, it is unlikely they are strong enough to hold the partnership together.

Goals that make a difference are the kind that both partner organizations can rally around. They point toward the purpose of the partnership and appeal to unique and strong ministry values. When you line them up they reveal the desired overall results of the partnership.

Goals that make a difference also take advantage of the unique capability and potential of the alliance. A big part of what makes any partnership worthwhile is the extent to which the collaboration leverages the competencies of each partner. True partnering goals show how the organizations combine their capabilities for maximum advantage.

As a whole, goals that make a difference will help answer the following questions:

- What difference will the alliance make in the ministry of the gospel?

- What does each partner gain?

- What skills, resources, and talents does each partner bring to the alliance?

Defining the goals of a partnership not only clarifies purpose and direction, it helps to spell out the benefits each party will gain. The more partners know about what each needs and stands to gain, the better able *they* will be to convert vision into practice.

What Each Partner Has to Offer and to Gain

Every organization enters into partnership for its own interests. This fact makes it essential that partners operate with a clear picture of what each seeks to gain from the relationship. The more ways a partnership bestows benefits, the more robust it is likely to be.

Discovering mutual advantage is a prerequisite for building a shared vision. The very notion of partnership suggests a two-way flow of potential benefits. Without it there is no reciprocity, and reciprocity is what differentiates partnership from paternalism, and healthy dependency from unhealthy dependency.[9] The only way to know whether or not a relationship is reciprocal is to determine what is in it for each partner.

Organizations that assess why they want to enter into this kind of relationship, what they can bring to it, and what they need to gain from it are in the best position to capture the power of shared vision.

The Limits of Shared Vision

Someone wisely said, "Life is what happens while you are planning it." The same is true of shared vision. While there is no getting around the necessity of clear goals and expectations, I don't want to leave the impression that you need it all up front like a blueprint. Building shared vision is not like constructing a building. It is more like putting together a team to win a game of soccer. What really counts is not a perfect game plan, but a team of players who have a desire to win and the skill to play. In other words, shared vision is not static but dynamic. It is a process that must be purposeful but not rigid, responsive to change but not driven by change. Ironically, the more you clarify and re-clarify goals and expectations as you go, the more the partnership is able to adjust to new directions, new learning, and new challenges.

2

Compatibility

Compatibility? Isn't allegiance to Christ and the work of the gospel ample common ground on which to build a partnership? Well, yes, in some ways. But it can also be the biggest barrier. At one level, it is easy to be cordial, even bighearted, with people who share your basic beliefs and values. But when it comes to sharing power, resources, and responsibilities, it takes a whole new level of common ground. Finding out what you hold in common takes time, but failure to do so is like building a house without a foundation.

Agreement on the Fundamentals

While agreement on fundamental beliefs is the most obvious aspect of compatibility, it is also the most easily overlooked. "Do two walk together unless they have agreed to do so?" asked God of a disloyal people (Amos 3:3). The obvious answer is no. If you want God to walk with you, you must walk with him. So it is in partnership. If you want to work together, you must be in agreement on several foundational issues.

At the very minimum, fundamental beliefs, values, and aspirations should be in the same universe. Partners must have the same convictions about God, Christ, the Holy Spirit, the gospel, and the Bible. Major differences cannot be glossed over. They will eventually surface and may put the whole partnership at risk. It is important to identify differences early on and to assess their potential impact on the partnership. On the other hand, it's not helpful to scrutinize theological positions too closely. There will surely be differences that merit debate. In such matters the old axiom applies: Unity in primary things, liberty in the secondary, and charity in all things. It is important to be completely clear with each other about the primary things.

Doctrinal statements are typically used to compare theological positions. The statement of the World Evangelical Alliance is widely used.[10] Public endorsement of well-known statements, such as the *Lausanne Covenant*[11] and *The Gospel of Jesus Christ: An Evangelical Celebration,*[12] also provides a handy index on one's theological frame of reference.

The best proof of an organization's beliefs is its reputation and track record. We are all adept at saying what we believe, but our actions eventually reveal what we truly value. Effective partners take as much time as necessary to investigate where the prospective partner invests its resources and how it conducts its ministry.

Compatibility in Operational Values and Ministry Priorities

Compatibility is also a function of having common ground in operational values and ministry priorities. While complete accord is important at the basic level of beliefs and values, compatibility is something more flexible. To be compatible means to be able to work together with a minimum of modification. Partners should not have to make major changes in operational values and priorities.

Operational values typically include financial practices, fundraising techniques, use of publicity, use of planning, approach to decision-making, management style, and so on. For example, consider the operational value of short-term teams of volunteers. An organization that places a high value on the role of short-term teams will have repeated difficulties with a partner that doesn't have this same priority and also some means of accommodating short-term teams. Partnership is much more difficult when one partner is required to make large operational changes. Also, change is easier when both partners share the same values.

The same goes for ministry priorities. Priorities should be compatible at the top. Otherwise lesser priorities get shoved aside, especially in uneven partnerships between large foreign agencies and relatively small local ministries. For instance, it's easy in principle to be supportive of church planting, but if the primary focus is social and economic development, the enormous effort it takes to actually plant churches may become a side issue. It doesn't take long for the agenda of a large relief and development agency to overshadow the priorities of a smaller indigenous church-planting ministry. In an effort to keep pace with the development agency, local priorities tend to take a back seat. In the same way, aggressive church planting agencies may unwittingly reshape the more holistic priorities of local ministries.

It's not an issue of development versus church planting. It's a matter of whose priorities dominate. If church planting is what a ministry wants to do, the best potential partners are generally those for whom church planting is the central priority. The more compatible the top priorities, the more smoothly the partnership is likely to run.

Consider Managerial Style

On the surface compatibility in managerial style can sound impractical. After all, we're talking about intercultural partnerships where differences in style are likely to be vast. Such differences require a great deal of cross-cultural understanding and skill. There is, however, more to compatibility than intercultural differences. The nature and purpose of the partnership also plays an important role. Highly integrated partnerships, where members from each organization work closely side-by-side, require a high level of compatibility. The need for compatibility in managerial style increases with the level of integration between partners (Figure 2.1).

Figure 2.1. One Model for Matching Compatibility to Task Integration

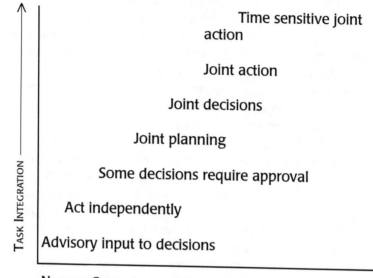

Partners don't have to work side-by-side to run into conflicts over managerial style. New, startup ministries are often more innovative and flexible than older, well-established ministries. Young ministries, like young people, are too fast for the adults to keep up. This is often the case in partnerships between pioneer ministries and established organizations. By their nature, pioneer ministries respond creatively to situations that are unfamiliar or unknown to conventional organizations. In partnership situations, the long-established organization should allow the pioneer ministry plenty of latitude in the relationship. Otherwise it will lose the advantage of having partnered with a pioneer ministry in the first place.

An Appreciation for Size and Capacity

It is easy to overlook size and capacity in assessing the compatibility of organizations. As Charles Taber observed, international partnerships can sometimes turn out like elephant-rabbit stew.[13]

When we use one elephant and one rabbit, it should not surprise us that the 50-50 stew tastes more of elephant than of rabbit! Small, local ministries in alliance with large, international organizations are at a decided disadvantage. A large organization may have a relatively low need—and therefore risk—in partnering with a small organization. The larger organization can more easily pull out of a relationship that no longer meets their needs. For the smaller organization, losing the partnership prematurely may be devastating.

One way to avoid this problem is to stay away from uneven relationships in the first place. Ideally, levels of need and risk should be similar enough so that both partners will benefit substantially, and thus have sufficient incentive to finish what they start. Another approach is to rely on other factors such as the Christian values of equality, justice, and brotherly love. For example, valuing the relationship in terms of what is good for the partner and not merely one's own agenda. But this, too, can be hazardous. Partners who collaborate primarily out of benevolence run the risk of overvaluing their contribution and undervaluing the partner's contribution. When that happens the overrated partner can easily fall into the trap of paternalism. To prevent this, partners should identify the reasons they are equally committed to the partnership, put it in writing, and revisit those reasons as the partnership evolves.

Another challenge of uneven relationships is the capacity to get things done. Large organizations may have staff members who work full-time in specialized areas, such as fundraising, training, or administration. They may underestimate what it is like in a small organization where each staff member has multiple jobs. For example, suppose a small, local ministry has agreed to host an educational institute together with a large, international agency. The large agency has one set of personnel for contributing to the educational design, and other staff for handling logistics. The local ministry, by contrast, has only a few people burdened with both responsibilities, and these same personnel have other duties in the organization. Unless partners understand such differences in capacity, they can easily set themselves up for failure.

This is not to suggest that differences in capacity are necessarily barriers to effective partnership. Differences are often the very factors that reveal how partners may complement one another. The point is, differences in the size and capacity of partner organizations need to be acknowledged and accounted for in how the work gets done. Although a partnership may be uneven in terms of the size and capacity of each organization, it need not be uneven in terms of the relative attention and effort each partner must contribute.

Confirming Common Ground

Can common ground between organizations happen intuitively? Absolutely! Should it happen without confirmation? Absolutely not! Even when prospective partners have known each other for many years, it is better to verify compatibility than to assume it. Each partner should be able to affirm or qualify compatibility in fundamental beliefs, operational values and priorities, and managerial style. They should also be aware of the implications of the size and capacity of each organization.

Establishing compatibility involves at least a modest level of research. Whether looking at a new potential partner or considering a joint venture with an old friend, there is much that one can easily overlook or forget. For this reason it helps to have a checklist of all the essential questions. One such checklist, *Partner Assessment and Selection,* is available in the back of this book (see Partnership Resources: One).

The best partnering relationships progress beyond doctrinal statements and organizational style and ask broader questions like, "Is the partnership simply supplementing each other's needs, or are we truly seeking what God is inviting us to do together?" But this doesn't always come easily. It requires that the partners think more broadly about what the collaboration can achieve in the work of the gospel. We must *grow* the common ground, not merely depend on finding it.

3

Ground Rules

Why can some partners pull together, tackle difficult ministries, and enjoy the relationship, while other partners can't? Even when partners have the necessary skills and are highly motivated, a partnership can be riddled with frustration and conflict.

One key to success is ground rules. Successful partners tend to have explicit guidelines that govern behavior. When partners follow the ground rules, they're better able to communicate effectively, share responsibility, resolve conflicts, and achieve joint action.

Ground rules define how each partner will engage with the other to achieve the goals of the partnership. They fix the limits of what you should and should not do. Collaboration doesn't happen in a vacuum; it needs a structure on which to operate. Ground rules provide that structure.

If you don't set ground rules, each party will operate by different, unstated rules. You will push forward under the false assumption that you understand each other. In any relationship this is dangerous. In cross-cultural partnerships it is fatal. The more effort you put into ground rules, the less time will be spent resolving disputes.

The five areas in which to establish ground rules are roles and responsibilities, communication, financial matters, conflict resolution, and disengagement.

Clear Roles and Responsibilities

Nothing disrupts a partnership more than a partner that doesn't fulfill its part of the bargain. That should never happen because a partner didn't know what it was expected to do. You can prevent that by identifying the basic roles and responsibilities of each partner.

The first step is to think through all the different roles that need to be performed. What must each partner do to provide full coverage of responsibilities to the partnership? Some common roles include project manager, fundraiser, bookkeeper, accountant, ministry specialist, and administrator. Out of these will flow specific responsibilities.

A good way to distinguish roles from responsibilities is to construct a matrix. List key personnel or related jobs in each organization across the top and the roles down one side. This helps you match each role with appropriate jobs. Have the partners work separately to identify who will do what. Then come together to compare your conclusions. Give time to explore differences and iron out any confusion. The sample matrix in Figure 3.1 can be adapted for your own use.

Figure 3.1 Roles Chart

Partnership Roles	Person Responsible	Person Responsible	Person Responsible

Systems for Sharing Information

Just as you need a clear picture of roles and responsibilities, you also need to know who needs what information and when. If partners are to make good decisions about the partnership, they need data about new projects, completed projects, fund transfers, ministry outcomes, special needs, and so forth. Information is to partnership what blood is to the human body. A healthy partnership has frequent and open communication in which information flows freely. Ground rules for information sharing help keep the channels open and responsive.

To develop an effective information system, ask the following questions:

- What are the key pieces of information we need to manage this partnership?

- What decisions do we need to make that require critical information?

- How might we go about collecting this information?

- What form should the data be put into for easy access and use?

Once you have identified what information is needed and by whom, you can outline communications guidelines. The guidelines need to identify who is responsible for communicating with whom, and to establish some do's and don'ts. At the very least you need to consider communication within your own organization, between the partners, and with donors.

These things don't have to be rigid or overly specific, but they do need to establish some basic parameters. The most important are that partners must be truly open with one another, that communication channels must be kept informal and spontaneous, and that important questions must be answered promptly. Here are some typical ground rules for information sharing:

- Establish written plans that clearly define the goals and action steps of the partnership.

- Persist in sharing information freely and in an undistorted manner.

- Appoint a representative from each organization to oversee all aspects of the partnership.

- Meet (monthly, quarterly, annually) to review the operations of the partnership and ensure that it is moving toward appropriate goals and fulfilling mutual aspirations.

- Provide (one, two, or three) reports per year updating the status and progress of joint projects.

- Propose new projects and changes to existing projects through a "project proposal form," and thereby avoid obligating one another to any project without previous written agreement.

Policies for Financial Accountability and Fundraising

Demonstrating financial integrity in missions partnerships has special challenges. Partners who are not clear about who does the fundraising and how it is done run the risk of confusing donors, or even of double dipping when each partner solicits the same donor for funds. Such an unintentional duplication of effort can quickly erode donor confidence. Suspicion about finances is especially acute when financial reporting is sloppy or vague. It is important not only to keep financial integrity before God but also to be perceived as doing so by others. A special challenge is adequate funding. Partners must be exceedingly clear whether funding is based on a budget or on a promise based on the charitable giving of others.

The easiest way to develop guidelines for financial accountability is by first asking yourselves a few basic questions:

- What financial information do we need?

- How will we keep track of funds related to joint projects?

- How can we best demonstrate financial integrity?

Second, make a list of what you need and expect from one another. Third, prioritize the list. Select the top five to seven items and restate each one as a guideline.

Repeat these three steps with regard to fundraising.

- Who is responsible for fundraising?

- How should donors be approached?

- Who should serve as the contact with the donor?

- How should projects be promoted?

Here are some standard guidelines for financial accountability and fundraising:

- Have funds sent to the organization and not to individuals.

- Transfer funds with utmost care, and send funds as designated by previous agreement.

- Do not obligate one another to any project without prior written agreement.

- Publish an audited financial report annually and send a copy to the partner.

- Permit one another to publicize the work and to provide the information necessary to gain interest and support.

- Promote and raise funds only for approved projects.

- Give a full explanation of your relationship in any publicity.

Handling Conflicts and Disagreements

There are no perfect partnerships. Unmet expectations, miscommunication, and cultural miscues are bound to create tensions. If you apply the principles of this book you can prevent many of these, but human nature being what it is, you can count on your fair share of conflicts and disagreements. It is neither helpful nor realistic to try to keep conflicts from occurring. A better way is to set up guidelines so that disputes are resolved without delay.

Addressing conflict immediately, however, doesn't necessarily mean relying on the direct, confrontational approach of Anglo-American culture. On the contrary, Americans are advised to use an indirect approach suitable to their partner's culture. Writing on how to handle conflict in cross-cultural ministry, Duane Elmer points out six critical perspectives.[14]

1. Most people in the world value relationships above other values. This is in bold contrast to American pragmatism that puts achievement first.

2. For most people, to criticize a person's words or acts constitutes an attack on the person and is seen as rude, if not vicious. Anglo-American partners who are quick to "tell it like it is" will succeed only at driving injury and alienation deeper.

3. Intercultural effectiveness begins by postponing judgment, asking questions, and taking a learning posture. Most people can easily read the difference between genuine respect and condescending tolerance.

4. Great care must be taken in making evaluative statements or comments that "place blame" on one person or group. Most Americans are not skilled at understanding people who express themselves indirectly.

5. While Anglo-Americans prefer a direct and frank reply, an indirect approach marked by deference, courtesy, and patience will accomplish far more in non-Western cultures.

6. The outsider should have a trusting friend in the host culture to act as a cultural interpreter and bridge-builder. A friend can be given permission to instruct you, give advice, and intervene on your behalf.

The challenge of cross-cultural conflict is immensely important and deserves more attention than I can give it here. For further study I recommend the book *Cross-Cultural Conflict: Building Relationships for Effective Ministry* by Duane Elmer. You will especially benefit from the principles listed in the last chapter of his book. Provided you have done your cross-cultural homework, ground rules such as these will help you resolve most issues:

- Handle any mix-up, mistake, or disagreement in a prayerful, courteous, and constructive manner.

- Consider a culturally appropriate way to broach the subject, preferring to assume the best of others, and to minimize any loss of face.

- Listen carefully to one another, to understand the concern, and to learn one another's perception of the problem. This includes asking open-ended questions in a non-accusatory way to fully understand the circumstances.

- Remain descriptive, citing what you know as opposed to what you surmise or suspect.

- Aim to meet the needs of both partners, and to state your needs clearly and forthrightly.

- Concentrate on fixing the future rather than rehashing the past and reopening old wounds.

- Accept responsibility when you have made a mistake, then make it right quickly, graciously, and generously.

Exit Procedures

Is your partnership forever? How will you know when it is over? For Western, goal-oriented partners, it is usually over when the objective is accomplished. For many non-Western partners it is never really over because it is a relationship, not a task. Even when the relationship has served its purpose, non-Western partners invariably strive to keep the relationship alive. This penchant for fraternal relationship is one of the wonderful gifts non-Western cultures have in abundance and Anglo-Americans sorely lack. Learning to live and work in community is one of the great benefits of intercultural partnership. Nevertheless, it may be legitimate for partners to move on, for their own benefit as well as the benefit of others. The question is how will you handle it when the time comes?

The time for separation may come because you anticipated it or it might be thrust upon you by unforeseen circumstances. Either way you will need an exit plan to minimize disruption to the partner organizations. Agreement on exit procedures is usually much easier to achieve when both organizations have the same general departure expectations and plan up front. To establish some mutual expectations, ask these questions:

- What are our assumptions about the duration of this relationship?

- Do we expect it to last forever or does it have an end point?

- How will we know when we have achieved our purpose?

- At what future points will we review the quality and results of the relationship?

- What would indicate that it might be time to modify or discontinue the partnership?

- What steps will we take to change or adjourn the partnership?

Whether or not you plan to stick together indefinitely, it is helpful to take the following actions:

- Identify the "deal breakers"—behaviors that would likely break up the partnership.

- Set firm dates for when you will sit down together and evaluate the meaning and impact of the partnership.

- Outline the steps you would take to close the partnership.

If it is appropriate, close on a high note, celebrate with fanfare and stories. The point of celebration is to mark the end of the partnership, and to do so with thanksgiving. Because Christians tend to view separation negatively, especially in the context of ministry, it may be seen as failure rather than success. Celebration can symbolize the positive nature of closure and of moving on to the next adventure. This doesn't have to be elaborate but it should be rich with compliments and stories of past achievement. The end of a partnership is a great opportunity to honor one another in an attitude of praise to God.

Some typical ground rules for disbanding a partnership include these:

- Evaluate the relationship at set intervals (or anticipated milestones) to determine the benefits of continuing.

- Consider possible dissolution of the partnership only after a thorough investigation of the apparent breach of agreement and necessary corrective action has been taken.

- Document the reasons for ending the partnership in a letter to the principals of the partner organization.

- Give advance warning that closure of the partnership is imminent and will be concluded by a set date.

Ground Rules that Work

For ground rules to be useful, partners must understand them and commit to using them. Understanding comes as you collaborate in formulating ground rules for your partnership.

First, keep it simple. A few ground rules stated clearly actually accomplish more than pages of detailed guidelines. It is almost certain that a long list of guidelines will be filed away and never seen again. A concise, relevant list is more likely to be used as a point of reference in continuing discussions and reviews. Do everything possible to make ground rules part of the operating assumptions of your relationship. They simply do not work otherwise.

Second, establish boundaries, not bureaucracy. It is easy to overdo it when it comes to making rules. Concerned about potential conflicts, some people start to think that if everyone follows the rules to the letter the relationship will be perfect. Before you know it guidelines become excessively complex and inflexible. In contrast, good guidelines are like road signs. They tell you where you are in the relationship and what to look out for. They set the boundaries for managing the relationship, but don't spell out procedures for every contingency.

Third, put it in writing. This is not the same as insisting on a contract. The purpose is not to ensure compliance but to avoid miscommunication and false assumptions. Written guidelines provide an objective point of reference in ongoing reviews and outcome evaluations.

To use ground rules effectively, partners must practice them regularly. One way is to refer to the rules before making decisions that affect your partner. For example, guidelines for fundraising might be reviewed before making plans to travel abroad to promote the ministry. Another way is to purposefully critique yourselves at the end of regular review meetings to identify how well you are using the rules and which ones you need to work on.

When all is said and done, ground rules foster cooperation by making operational expectations explicit. Making expectations clear-cut and mutually acceptable is the essential task of managing a partnership.

Checklist One

Discovering Shared Vision

Discovering shared vision means developing the guidance system for the partnership. To accomplish this, work through the following questions with your partner:

- [ ] Are we compatible in doctrinal beliefs, operational values, and ministry priorities?

- [ ] Do we have a clear sense of what partnering could potentially bring to both ministries?

- [ ] Do we feel that the conditions are right for partnering?

- [ ] Have we estimated what each of us must pay, in terms of costs and changes, to achieve the benefits of partnering?

- [ ] Are key personnel in each organization appointed and prepared to champion the partnership?

- [ ] Do we have goals that satisfy important values on both sides of the partnership?

- [ ] Have we defined clear mutual expectations about how we will work together?

- [ ] Are adequate systems in place to measure and track our progress?

Part Two: Relationship

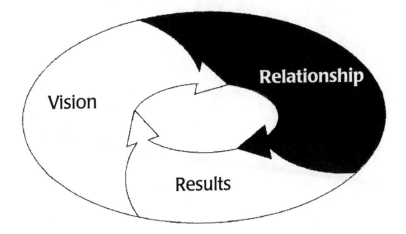

Vision

Relationship

Results

4

Alliance Champions

Partnership is nothing if it is not personal. It's all about relating. In the end it comes down to how people relate to each other and how they work together. Sounds simple. But in actuality the ability to work well together is the function of many factors such as shared values, trust, communications, expectations, competency, interpersonal skills, and cross-cultural skills, just to name a few. The most significant factors reside in individuals and the commitments they share. You may have a compelling strategy, state-of-the art technology, and a proven promotional plan, but you won't achieve real partnership if you don't have the right people involved and committed to the relationship.

Partnering organizations have to connect at the personal level, and this is best achieved through *alliance champions*. Alliance champions are the people most responsible for making the partnership work. This means that each organization must have at least one person dedicated to managing the relationship. Two alliance champions in place who have a strong bond of trust are the single most important ingredient for a successful partnership.

Although alliance champions may have slightly different roles depending on their particular type of partnership, they usually involve some degree of the following seven tasks.

Build Rapport

Connecting at the personal level doesn't mean that partners have to be close friends. In fact, intimate friends sometimes make the worst partners. Partnership doesn't require friendship, but it does require rapport.

Rapport is what you have when people come to know and appreciate one another. Under normal circumstances, rapport develops as people spend time together, get to know one another, and build a mutual history through common experiences. But intercultural partnerships have three tall hurdles to overcome: distance, culture, and language.

We'll discuss culture and language in the next chapter. For now let's consider the challenge of distance.

Partners who work side-by-side have a great advantage over partners who are geographically dispersed. When you work in the same place you have many occasions to exchange information and build relationships, and face-to-face interaction is crucial. The first step to building rapport is showing interest in others. People have to "see" you are interested in them, that you are paying special attention to their thoughts and well-being. That's hard to do without the benefit of nonverbal behavior and clues like tone of voice, pauses, emphasis on certain words, and contextual awareness. Partners who work at a distance have to figure out how to show interest without being present.

The lack of direct contact also makes it difficult to be responsive, which is the second step to building rapport. Rapport requires more than just words or positive feelings about people. Rapport develops as partners respond in concrete ways that demonstrate appreciation, respect, and understanding. For instance, a big part of showing respect is in how you interact with a person in the presence of others. When you have faith in a person's character or competence it can't help but show. The challenge is how to demonstrate confidence in others when you work at a distance.

When it comes right down to it, face-to-face meetings are virtually irreplaceable for building rapport, especially in the early stages of partnership. Phone calls and video conferencing can help maintain interpersonal bonds but they are not effective in creating them. Text-only technology, such as e-mail, simply cannot accommodate emotional and situational context. Partners must have time together—not just work time, but social time as well.

If your partnership does not involve resident personnel, someone has to travel. International travel, obviously, can be expensive and exhausting. One advantage to having an alliance champion in each organization is that they can share the travel requirements. That way four trips a year become two for each champion. Neither has to be away from home too long, and they have the invaluable experience of seeing life and ministry in each other's world.

Another way to beat the travel challenge is to have intensive time together, such as a planning retreat. A combination of planned interaction and free time to socialize can speed the process of getting to know one another and building history. Also, exercises such as personality style inventories can build common ground. And, of course, longevity helps. The longer partners work together, the more opportunities they have to build relationships.

Face-to-face meetings don't automatically lead to rapport, however. Global partners must be intentional about building relationships. That is the first duty of the alliance champion.

Provide Leadership

In addition to being the main relational link, alliance champions are also the visible leaders of the partnership, serving in both coordination and advocacy roles.

As coordinators, alliance champions are responsible to represent the interests of their organization and make sure the goals of the partnership are reconciled and integrated with the mission and strategy of their own organization. They also have management responsibilities, such as creating shared vision, developing guidelines, building trust, and measuring results.

As advocates, alliance champions are responsible for gaining the approval of senior management, securing resource allocations, and ensuring that the appointing organization keeps its promises. Champions also have a vision-casting function: They need to be able to explain the joint venture simply and power-fully and to convey the excitement, challenge, and opportunity of the partnership to diverse audiences. They are responsible for effectively representing not only their appointing organization but also the partner organization to donors and other stake-holders of the joint venture.

Above all, alliance champions live the partnership and come to personify it. They are not merely agents representing the interests of their respective organizations. In the end it is personal, passionate leadership that separates ministry partnerships from business transactions.

Clarify Expectations

Alliance champions specify and design the expectations of the relationship. Partnerships are undermined when partners work under different assumptions about *when* results will be achieved or *what* those results should be. Alliance champions collaborate to keep their respective organizations on the same page.

Clarifying expectations is not something alliance champions do only at the outset of the relationship. Because expectations are never entirely clear and are almost constantly in a state of change, the role continues.

Early expectations are always fuzzy and speculative. That's the nature of getting started. It's also why a partnership needs clear, formal leadership. It takes leadership to define goals, clarify boundaries, and focus attention on shared values. Even at that, intercultural differences can impose new assumptions. For example, how does one integrate expectations between African partners who want to start the process by building relationships and Anglo-American partners who want to cut to the chase and move directly toward measurable objectives?

Alliance champions should be aware that defining expectations poses a strange irony. The more precisely expectations are defined, the more likely they will change. Conversely, broadly stated expectations are less likely to change, simply because they allow more latitude. Alliance champions must find the middle ground between machine precision and wishful thinking.

Keep Things Simple

Alliance champions should insist on simplicity in plans and written agreements. I have found that when plans are filled with tightly defined objectives and meticulous guidelines, partnerships falter. Overly specific objectives trap partners on a one way street in a world that demands flexibility and quick response. Champions don't use goals to force things to happen. They use them as points of reference to manage change. When partners don't hit their targets, champions collaborate to either change the target or the strategy. Champions keep the partnership flexible by keeping it simple.

You can work very hard in an effort to get everything just right in the partnership. But it rarely works that way. It's better to work on being flexible, forbearing, and focused. Mutual encouragement in the faith (not flawless plans) lies at the heart of successful partnership in the gospel.

Keep Communications Flowing

Intercultural partners often have trouble getting accurate information from distant sites, especially bad news. Alliance champions must be keenly aware of the information flow patterns of the partner organization and how to get around inadequacies. When it comes to communications between partners, alliance champions are like plumbers: They not only fix clogged pipes, they ensure that the communication systems are designed to handle the increased flow of information.

For example, a common clogged pipe effect is in financial reporting. I have often found it necessary to help a partner organization improve its bookkeeping and accounting system. It does no good to require a partner to provide specific financial reports when it doesn't have the ability to get it done. Global partnerships often involve improving organizational capacity.

Go the Distance

Alliance champions hold on in spite of frustrations and setbacks. It is their job to see the partnership through the rough spots.

They don't look for a way out when things get tough. They look for a way through. If we view relationships as disposable, it's hard to have Christian partnership. Commitment, not friendliness, reflects the true nature of Christian partnerships.

Creating and managing a ministry partnership takes time. Significant impact in the work of the gospel often will not be felt for months or even years. Champions must know this and have the determination to hold on in the meantime. It takes a sincere and deep belief in what the partnership stands for and in its ultimate goals. More importantly it takes self-sacrificing humility and love to stay with it when things go wrong and expectations go unmet.

The best partnerships are like long-term investments: The markets may go up and down, but in the long run it's all gain. People who pump money into ministries and run off at the first sign of trouble know nothing of partnership, not to mention stewardship. Alliance champions must be willing to accept the hardship of ministry and endure with patience the fears and injuries of the long haul.

Partners who struggle together through difficulties develop a new forbearance, a fastidious allegiance. While modern society has mastered the art of avoiding hardship, the Scriptures portray suffering as one of the greatest sources of blessing and growth (Romans 5:3; 2 Corinthians 4:17). The idea of commitment has no higher expression than fellowship in suffering (Philippians 3:10). Let partners struggle with external threats to the ministry or face a sudden tragedy, and those very frustrations that threaten the relationship will bring the loyalty that only true partners can know.

Keep God at the Center

In a very real sense God is the third party in any ministry partnership. Indeed, God is the *principal* partner and the one whose concerns and interests must be weighed in every decision. Unless you are attending to this partnership with God, no amount of effort will produce the fruit of the gospel (John 15:1–17).

Alliance champions have to be deliberate about keeping God at the center of the relationship.

It is all too easy, and too common, to get caught up in the business of partnering and forget the one for whom the partnership exists in the first place. It is easy to assume that because it is a "Christian ministry" God is automatically involved. Organizations of all kinds have carried on, blissfully ignorant that God has left the building.

A crucial role of the alliance champion is the habit of letting God in on every detail of the relationship. This involves being avid in prayer personally and corporately when the partners meet. It means taking time to think theologically about your strategies, methods, and partnering behaviors. It also means thoughtfully evaluating ministry outcomes and their meaning to the work of the gospel. All the material in this book about setting goals and measuring results is less about using good management practices than about understanding what God is inviting you to do, then looking to see if it's happening and what you can learn from it. Setting direction and checking progress provide vital feedback to help realign your daily experience with your eternal beliefs.

Thinking theologically about the ministry and the partnership is what will keep you biblically faithful and missionarily effective.

Support the Needs of the Alliance Champions

The international and cross-cultural context places a unique set of constraints on the champion's work. For starters, the distances involved demand a more sophisticated and mobile electronic toolkit to plan and execute their work. While champions may rarely see one another, they have to stay in touch regularly— both with each other and with their respective organizations— via electronic conferencing.

Alliance champions must discover the methods and technologies that will enable them to establish a rhythm in communications. There are so many obstacles: switching time zones, difficulties getting in touch with remote partners, lack of regular meetings, and unclear direction. Distant champions will benefit by being able to plan and organize their work and travel around a structured pattern of communication. Rhythm in communications, whether through telephone, e-mail, or teleconferencing, will improve integration between local and distant alliance champions.

Rhythm in planning and review cycles will also enable champions to avoid the trap of excessive travel and ensure that face-to-face meetings are used to their fullest advantage. Because face-to-face meetings are so powerful and satisfying, it seems easier to just show up and meet than to work the disciplines of regular communication, planning, and review. Champions can easily exceed their personal endurance and their budgets if they try to make up for deficiencies by more frequent travel.

Although alliance champions live the partnership and even personify it, they cannot do the job alone. Alliance champions must have an interdisciplinary group that represents every relevant function within the partner organizations. For example, a resource team might include a key person from finance, one from fundraising, and another from a specific ministry program. Whether or not resource people operate as a self-directed team is not the issue. What is important is that they know they are part of a group that is responsible for a particular partnership. It is only when a team of people from both organizations is working together—frequently, informally, and inclusively—that partnering can take hold between ministry organizations.

Qualities of the Alliance Champion

The quality of a partnership rests on the quality of the people charged with making it work. Alliance champions should posses the qualifications required of any missionary, such as a living faith in Christ, humility, adaptability, compassion, a genuine interest in others, a willingness to serve, and a bias for cooperation.

So where do you start when selecting champions? The best place is with the main biblical texts that develop the requirements of leaders: 1 Timothy 3:1–13, 2 Timothy 2:1–13, Titus 1:5–9, Acts 6:1–6, and Exodus 18:21–22.

There are also a variety of qualities alliance champions need in order to succeed as partnership facilitators:

- A realistic view. This means an understanding of how intercultural partnerships work. Ambiguity in partnerships is the norm. Only rarely does everything go right and fall into place at the right time.

- A political sense. This is the politics of how things get done in partnerships. People cooperate when it is in their interest to do so. An alliance champion has to know what is in it for the partner as well as for his own organization.

- Poise under fire. Champions periodically come under fire from different groups—sponsoring churches, major donors, senior management, and other colleagues. The mature mind handles criticism quietly and efficiently, with a minimum of disruption.

- A sense of honor. Alliance champions are privy to the faults and foibles of the partner organization and their personnel. It takes a genuine respect and love for the partner to avoid divulging sensitive information inappropriately.

- Creative thinking. Of all partnership problems, people problems are usually the toughest to resolve. Alliance champions must have an extra amount of patience and tact, be able to dialogue well, and be willing to consult before taking action.

While written guidelines and goals are essential tools of all types of partnerships, they remain just that. They cannot substitute for the human interactions that constitute the real substance of global partnering. There must be plenty of contact between the partnering organizations, and access to people who can make the partnership happen. Alliance champions are the main personal link. They provide the strong bond of trust and communication that will allow a partnership to get off the ground.

5
Intercultural Understanding

Anyone experienced in intercultural ministry will immediately recognize that an American wrote this book. The thinking style and approach to the whole subject of partnering is distinctly Anglo-American.[15] For instance, I start with the idea that vision is imperative to effective partnership. That there should be a vision and that its clarification should serve as a guide to partnering represents at least three American assumptions, according to Edward T. Hall and Mildred Reed Hall in *Understanding Cultural Differences.*

One underlying assumption is that the present is oriented to the future. Vision is possible because the American concept of time is linear and moves from the present to the future. For us, time can be segmented and used to build incrementally toward a desired image of the future. In some cultures, time is a cycle from the present to the past. They rely on tradition for guidance.

Another assumption is that change is possible and desirable. The American idea of progress inclines us to master a situation and change it. In traditional cultures, change is often viewed as negative and disruptive to society.

The idea that vision is an imperative reveals the American, and generally Western, propensity to organize ideas into laws, principles, or some type of cause/effect relationship. Although it makes perfect sense to Americans, it doesn't equate in cultures where concrete situations, not abstract ideas, are the organizing principles of life.

These cultural differences are only the beginning of why this book is culture-bound. Every one of the nine imperatives of partnership represents Anglo-American cultural patterns. And so it should be. Coming from my perspective, I can hardly be expected to do otherwise. That is not to say there is no room for adjustment and accommodation to other cultures. Americans have a great deal to learn from other cultures and the more we do so the more we are enriched as human beings. Indeed, the purpose of this chapter is to draw attention to the importance of culture learning and accommodation.

The way this book is constructed reflects my cultural heritage. And awareness of that fact is the first step to intercultural understanding. Culture matters, and global partners must take it seriously. If ever we hope to collaborate with the servants of God in another culture, we have to be aware of our culture as well as theirs.

A Conviction that Culture Matters

This fact was never clearer than when I lived in East Africa. Although I had studied urban sociology in the multicultural city of San Francisco and had traveled in several countries of Asia, the power of culture didn't sink in until I had to grapple with it on a daily basis. I quickly discovered that Africans did not operate with the same set of rules I brought with me from California. All the normal ways of gathering information, managing tasks, and making decisions no longer applied. I needed answers to practical questions, and fast. How does authority work? How are decisions made? By what criteria is success judged? How does information flow between people and levels in organizations?

In search of answers I sought the counsel of African friends, and looked for clues in African literature. After digging through volumes of material on African philosophy, religion, and anthropology, several features of traditional African styles of thinking emerged. Taken together the features provided a simple framework for thinking about what I was encountering. The framework did not answer all my questions but it did help me formulate explanations and anticipate possible disconnects.

For example, when I had trouble getting feedback on the status of a project, it was because I was relying too much on written reports. In Africa, information flow is relationship-based. I could wait for weeks for an overdue written report, but if I showed up in person the ministry leader would give me his undivided attention and I would learn everything I needed to know. As long as I maintained personal contact I could tap the flow of information.

A Commitment to Learn Culture

Anyone who wants to have a global partnership but who has never lived outside his or her culture is at a distinct disadvantage. For one thing, people are only a little more conscious of their own culture than they are of the air they breathe. Only those who have been out of their culture for an extended period of time discover their need for it. With all my training, I didn't really see my cultural expectations until they didn't work for me anymore. In order to understand how my African colleagues communicated, made decisions, and solved problems, I had to realize how I did those things.

Would-be intercultural partners who have not had the advantage of extensive cross-cultural experience must proceed with caution. Achieving intercultural understanding takes time—a lot of time. Books, seminars, and missions trips are helpful, but they only provide a starting point. Nothing less than long-term commitment and learning from experience will lead to cultural competence.

In today's world, with so many people crisscrossing the globe, it may seem that some people do just fine without extensive cross-cultural experience. A closer look, however, will almost certainly reveal a great deal of cultural accommodation. Unfortunately most of it is one-directional. Non-Western ministries almost routinely accommodate to Western partners. There are several explanations that may seem reasonable: English is the language of global business, the influence of the West on the world economy, and the fact that many top ministry leaders are educated in the West. But none of these reasons reflect the Christ-like attitude of humility. The global use of the English language, for instance, may be an opportunity to leverage the gospel, but not at the expense of esteem for others and brotherly love. The exclusive use of English may communicate a lack of respect and signal an attitude of paternalism. Even a minimal effort to use the local language will demonstrate a commitment to the relationship. Christians operate best not from the position of power, but from humility and deference to others. The way to show humility is by learning your partner's culture and moving at least halfway across the cultural divide.

An Understanding of Culture

Appreciating the nature of culture and its pervasive influence on our lives is the first ingredient of intercultural understanding. When we understand how culture works, we have a framework for thinking about specific cultures.

Culture is the shared ways in which groups of people understand and interpret the world. It implies a measure of "likeness" in ways of thinking, knowing, and acting. And people like it that way. Culture touches everything that has anything to do with how human beings see, hear, and perceive the world. Nothing is known that is not sifted through the meaning filters of culture.

The *Willowbank Report on Gospel and Culture* defines culture as follows:

> Culture is an integrated system of beliefs (about God or reality or ultimate meaning), of values (about what is true, good, beautiful and normative), of customs (how to behave, relate to others, talk, pray, dress, work, play, trade, farm, eat, etc.), and of institutions which express these beliefs, values and customs (government, law courts, temples or churches, family, schools, hospitals, factories, shops, unions, clubs, etc.), which binds a society together and gives it a sense of identity, dignity, security, and continuity.[16]

To acknowledge culture and insist that it must be taken seriously is not the same as endorsing all cultural norms and expressions. Culture is man-made; as such it is a mixture of good and evil. As the *Lausanne Covenant* states, "Because man is God's creature, some of his culture is rich in beauty and goodness. Because he is fallen, all of it is tainted with sin and some of it is demonic."[17]

There is plenty in every culture to admire as well as to disdain. Newcomers, however, may not see this. It is important that they postpone judgment about what might be good or bad. More often than not, the newcomer's judgment is more a reflection of his own cultural blind spots than of wisdom. Discernment is best achieved by seeking the counsel of local Christian leaders.

Culture can be partly understood by thinking of it in layers. Donald Smith suggests that culture is like an onion.[18] The visible outer layer is comprised of the observable features of a society such as language, architecture, food, shrines, and art. Yet while these are all part of the culture they do not define the culture. They are merely the symbols of a deeper level of culture. By way of analogy, the clothing you wear may say something about you, but not much. It would be disappointing if others were to judge your character by your clothing. You could rightly claim that they don't know you enough to make any statements about who you are. In the same way, we know virtually nothing about another culture by outward appearances. To understand it we have to move beyond the obvious.

The next layer—or more accurately, layers—are the norms and values of a culture. Like an onion the various layers merge into one another. It is difficult to know where norms begin and values end. Norms are a collective sense of what is right and wrong. They show up in a wide range of formal and informal standards, from laws to table etiquette. Norms are ways of thinking and acting that are accepted throughout the society by common consent and enforced by social pressure. In this way norms create a sense of stability and predictability in a society. Consequently, those who break from the norm may be viewed as threatening and destabilizing to the order of things.

The core of culture represents the accumulated values and behavior that arise from society's most basic assumptions and beliefs. As Smith notes, "These come from the accumulated experience of a society, explanations and actions that seem to have worked for the society's survival. They interpret puzzling phenomena and provide an understanding of the ultimate mysteries of life, death, and eternity. These values seem necessary for maintaining the group and life itself."[19] This is the most powerful level of culture, and it is the most permanent.

Seeing culture in multiple layers suggests something of its complexity. Overlay one culture with another, or with multiple cultures, and the complexity increases geometrically. To achieve understanding it is necessary to "peel away" the layers of culture to find the core values, beliefs, and assumptions. Consequently, culture learning is a long and difficult path.

People who focus on a particular ministry in a particular cultural context over a long period of time stand the greatest chance of enjoying effective intercultural communication.

An Understanding of Self as Well as Others

So how do you approach intercultural understanding? It comes through learning in three areas: your own culture, the partner's culture, and your own personal traits and behavioral tendencies. All three are essential to cultural competence.

Understand your own culture. The first part of intercultural competence is being aware that your own behavior is influenced by basic cultural assumptions, values, and beliefs. Being familiar with the origins of your own behavior is no less important than understanding the new culture. In fact, it is extremely difficult to figure out another culture without understanding something of your own. The problem is that one's approach to thinking, deciding, and communicating is so natural it is hard to imagine life any other way. As I discovered in East Africa, the best way to see one's own culture is in comparison to other cultures. If you want to learn other cultural patterns, you must be able to distinguish them from your own cultural patterns.

Understand the partner's culture. The second part of intercultural competence is familiarity with the dominant ways of thinking and acting in the host culture. This means much more than mere familiarity with traits you can see such as clothing, food, mannerisms, and social etiquette. True understanding comes when you can connect specific behaviors to underlying assumptions, values, and beliefs. This involves enough study and experience to understand the various layers of a particular culture and then to function comfortably within it.

Ostensibly, intercultural understanding is the ability to see the world as other people see it. But the truth is, no one who crosses a major barrier of culture will see the world in quite the same way. For example, David comes from the Kamba tribe in Kenya, East Africa. He was educated in Canada and the United States and holds a Ph.D. from a major American university. Although David has used English since childhood and has worked alongside Europeans and North Americans his entire adult life, he says he must still work to understand and relate to Americans. With all of his training and experience, David is still very much African. And, frankly, we can thank God for it. The gifts David brings, as an African (and as a Christian) is what makes a relationship with him rich and meaningful.

The purpose of intercultural understanding is not to become *like* the host culture, but to communicate with a minimum of distortion and have the ability to honor your relationships and obligations.

Understand your personal style. Understanding your own personal style can make a big difference in how you respond to particular properties of a new culture. My wife, for example, thrives in situations where relationships are the key to getting around. For her, living in Africa came easy. For me, it was all work. My personal style is more results-oriented than people-oriented. The differences in our personal styles made a difference in our cross-cultural experience.

Numerous personality "tests" are available to help you find your own style. Two popular ones are listed below:

The *Personal DISCernment Inventory* (PDI) provides a general and detailed description of your particular behavioral style, and assists you in developing a comprehensive list of both strengths and weaknesses that help or hinder your effectiveness in various settings. PDI is available in several languages. For information contact: Team Resources, Inc., Atlanta, Georgia, USA.

The *Myers-Briggs Type Indicator* (*MBTI*) is one of the most commonly used instruments. It requires a trained, certified facilitator to interpret the results. For information contact: Center for Applications of Psychological Type, Gainesville, Florida, USA.

The best use of a personality style instrument is in relationship to other people. You will benefit more if your partners also complete the instrument so that you can compare findings. It will then be possible to anticipate the best use of everyone's style, and how to prevent and minimize unproductive conflict.

Another aspect of culture learning, of course, is language. If at all possible, partners should be willing to learn the language of the local culture. Language competency is vital if you are to enter the culture and work fluently in it. Certainly you can get by for short engagements without real fluency, but "getting by" won't allow for the kind of in-depth involvement that the best partnerships enjoy. If you can't make the commitment to learn the language, then rely on someone who can.

Strategies for Learning Culture

The ideal way to learn culture may be as varied as personal learning styles. Nevertheless, experience has taught us a few basic strategies.

Proceed from general to specific. A proven sequence for culture learning is to move from general to specific. For instance, if you had to trek through an unfamiliar forest it would be a terrific advantage to first view it from high up in an airplane. In a similar way it helps to start with a view of culture in general, then a broad view of your culture and the new culture in comparison, and finally specifics of the new culture and how your personality style is likely to interact with it.

Learn by doing. Experience is the best teacher—or more accurately, *guided* experience is the best teacher. The way to learn a new culture is to be immersed in it. Culture is holistic, tied in to every facet of life. Therefore culture learning must also be holistic—under the influence of all the physical, emotional, relational, and social forces that ebb and flow together in everyday life. That is not to suggest that you simply dive blindly into another culture. Effective learning requires a guide, a cultural mediator or mentor.

Unfortunately, learning from experience takes years, and few of us have the advantage of a skilled mentor. Even with an able coach at our side, culture learning is too complex to leave it to serendipity. To complicate matters, we often find ourselves working with multiple cultures in today's global neighborhood.

Learn by comparison. The best way to supplement experience is through the comparison of cultures. The comparative approach is more efficient than relying on experience alone and it contributes much to removing the mystery of cultural diversity. One thing that makes culture learning difficult is the level of mystery. In cross-cultural encounters things occur for which there is no apparent explanation, that is, no explanation from one's own cultural background. When the mind has nothing familiar with which to assign meaning it grabs the most convenient memory. This can result in false impressions and misjudgments. Some of the mystery can be removed through comparison of major cultural patterns.

While culture has many dimensions, some are core systems in all cultures. These "core systems" make it possible to compare widely differing cultures from a single vantage point. For example, in *The Dance of Life*, Edward T. Hall compares French, German, and American culture through their concepts of time. This one dimension—time—provides a lens through which to compare different cultures.

A number of researchers have compared cultures by viewing them through different dimensions. I particularly recommend the work of Mary O'Hara-Devereaux and Robert Johansen in

Globalwork: Bridging Distance, Culture and Time. Others include Edward T. Hall and Mildred Reed Hall (1990), Fons Trompenaars (1994), and Geert Hofstede (1984).

Important as it is, culture learning through comparison is not enough. In fact, it can be downright risky. General ideas of cultural patterns can harden into stereotypes. Unless we are guarded in the use of comparisons, we can easily fall into the trap of attributing certain traits without really getting to know people. The way to avoid such pitfalls is by getting involved with people and building relationships. The bonds of relationship supply the emotional will to break past generalizations. When we truly respect and appreciate others we are less inclined to settle for labels and oversimplifications.

Build relationships. Relationships afford the richest opportunities for learning culture. It is within relationship with people that cultural differences come to the surface. Without deepening trust relationships, outsiders are left stranded without explanations or guides to the local culture.

The final component of learning culture is a matter of the heart. It is not tolerance for differences that creates intercultural understanding. It is affection for people. Humility, respect, and love are what move us from conceptual understanding to instinctive behaviors that bridge cultural diversity. It is humility that puts us at liberty to learn from those we don't understand. It is respect that enables us to defer to others even when their behavior is irritating. And it is love that keeps us caring, even when the stereotype is true.

Like any good relationship, intercultural understanding is not an end. It is a journey. And it only happens when partners take the journey together.

6
Mutual Trust

The goal of building relationships and creating intercultural understanding is mutual trust. Partnerships are built on trust. Without it, they simply don't work.

Trust is what allows us to accept at face value what others say. We don't have to worry about hidden agendas or distortion. We can act on the information without fear that we might later regret it. We don't have to check up on one another or question every variation from what was expected. Trust allows us to share information with each other freely and openly, even negative information. With trust the whole process of making decisions, and taking action becomes much simpler. Trust allows us to devote more attention to the ministry than we could in a climate of suspicion. It makes relationships easier, less demanding, and more rewarding.

However, trust poses a dilemma. While it is the most powerful component of a partnership, it is also the most fragile. A partnership can no more function without trust than a body can function without a brain. Although the brain is in charge of the body, everything it knows depends on the body. In a similar way, trust exists only where there is shared vision, compatibility, supportive relationships, intercultural understanding, and meaningful results.

As I have suggested throughout this book, partnership is about managing expectations. If you manage them well, you will simultaneously build trust because trust is composed of expectations—more precisely, the *positive* expectations we have of others. Simply stated, we trust those who meet our expectations. We assume they will act in ways consistent with our interests. In contrast, distrust arises when those on whom we depend appear unwilling or unable to meet our expectations.

There are, however, different levels of trust and different sources of trust.

Levels of Trust

Different types of relationships require different degrees of trust. The need for trust moves along a sliding scale, as suggested in Figure 6.1. The level of trust needed depends on the level of interdependence in the relationship. The cultural distance between the partners also affects the need for trust. As a rule, the need for trust rises as the level of interdependence rises. The more partners are dependent upon each other, the more they need trust. The further apart partners are in language and culture, the more they need trust.

Partnerships face the highest levels of interdependence because the organizations are more highly intertwined. If something goes wrong, each organization loses. Indeed, the power of partnership is not only in combined strength, but also in shared risk. It takes far more trust to face hardship together than to succeed together. Ministries whose dignity, significance, and hope are at some level dependent upon one another require deep reservoirs of trust.

In contrast, relationships that require little task integration are less dependent upon each other and have less need of trust. For example, small one-time grants require the least amount of trust. The risk to the grantor is that the project might prove to be a dud or the funds might be mishandled. In either case, the damage would amount to the loss of funds and the loss of face. Such a loss would call for corrective action to be sure, but the damage could be more easily repaired than if resources, power,

Figure 6.1 Levels of Trust

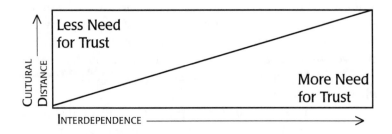

and responsibilities were intertwined, as they are in a partnership. The risk to the recipient is that the grant may not be awarded or the project might be derailed. Either way the risk is no greater than the ministry would face if it were to seek other sources of funding.

The more partnering organizations become interdependent, the more they need trust. While low integration can be managed through written contracts, high integration calls for high trust.

Sources of Trust

In a study of sixty-five business partnerships, William Bergquist and colleagues found three kinds of trust in a partnership: trust in intentions, trust in competency, and trust in perspectives.[20] We trust people when we are convinced they are interested in our well-being or in the well-being of the ministry in which we are involved together. We trust people when they demonstrate they have the capacity to benefit us or our ministry. We are also inclined to trust people who share our perspectives and see the world in the same way we do. By contrast, we don't trust people who act in ways that don't seem to be in our best interests. Trust erodes when people prove incompetent or powerless to fulfill the expectations we have of them. And most of us find it hard to trust people who do not share our basic beliefs and values.

Bergquist also found that trust in partnerships couldn't develop fully unless all three kinds of trust—intentions, competency, perspectives—are present and active. For instance, partners with strong shared perspectives and genuine concern will not hold our trust if they are incapable of fulfilling their promises. In this case we may regard them as unworthy of trust not because they are malicious but simply because they can't deliver. And so it is with the other kinds of trust as well. Having two out of the three kinds is usually not enough to sustain trust. It builds when all three areas are in play, and it erodes when one or more are missing.

Trust is not something that happens by accident. It is crafted on purpose, with each partner's full awareness of how his or her actions affect the relationship. Given that we trust those who demonstrate they are worthy of it, the best way to create trust is by being trustworthy. In other words, we create trust not so much by trusting others as by giving others reasons to trust us. There are three ways to build trust, according to Robert Bruce Shaw in *Trust in the Balance:* demonstrating concern, acting with integrity, and achieving results. To that list I add a fourth: a willingness to risk.

A Willingness to Risk

Trust comes with a price. It involves risk. People don't always live up to our expectations of them. In fact, trust and risk are interrelated. Thus, the first source of trust is a willingness to risk.

The more we trust, the more vulnerable we become. An organization that cannot live with vulnerability should not expect to succeed at partnering. Cooperation requires trust, and trust makes you vulnerable. An organization that cannot trust others will end up imposing a system of strict policies and procedures that invariably institutionalize distrust, forcing partners to either comply or face punishment. This is very different from establishing general ground rules as described in Chapter 3. Admittedly, even ground rules can be mishandled and used to enforce compliance rather than establish boundaries. When that happens trust erodes, giving way to still more formalization.

In short, trying to ensure success in partnership through rigid rules and regulations simply doesn't work. Like too much cholesterol in the blood, too many rules and regulations clog the flow of information and limit individual creativity and initiative. The more people depend on policies and procedures, the less they trust each other. That's why ministries without trust lack the agility to keep pace with rapidly changing situations. Variations in their expectations are met with suspicion because they don't fit neatly within the rules and regulations. As a consequence, where suspicion grows, the cost of partnership escalates.

Without trust, partners become unwilling or unable to be completely open with each other; especially about problems. A sure sign of distrust is an inability to bring difficult issues to the surface and work through them. Without trust, people focus more on their own agendas than on listening to their partners and on building collaborative solutions.

Without trust, people second-guess decisions and fail to support each other in joint tasks. They do what they feel is in the interest of their appointing organization rather than in the interest of the partnership.

The cost of suspicion is high indeed. On the other hand, trust drives down the cost of partnering because it keeps communications open, fosters a capacity for action, and enhances collaboration. Yet none of this is possible without risk. Someone has to take the first step to build trust, and that invariably involves risk.

Concern for the Well-Being of Others

Have you noticed how enthusiastically people respond when you take on *their* agenda? Show people you care and they will begin to trust you almost immediately. It takes more than that to sustain trust, of course. But for starters, nothing bonds you more quickly than taking on the needs and interests of others.

This isn't the kind of concern that merely sees others as needy. Genuine concern for the well-being of others is not the antiseptic sentimentality of those who, from a safe distance, give out of their wealth in order to feel good about themselves. People who truly care for others share their load and borrow their discomfort. They do not see others as merely needy, but as neighbors, fellow members of humanity, and if Christians, as co-laborers in the gospel.

The kind of concern that generates trust is more than empathy. It's obviously important to be aware of and sensitive to the feelings of others. But if you hope to create trust, concern has to be acted upon. Trust comes from acting in ways that help meet another's needs.

In earlier chapters we discussed some of the ways to demonstrate concern, such as discovering shared vision, sorting out priorities, developing ground rules, and building rapport. Getting to know your partners and building rapport is also indispensable. It is difficult to demonstrate concern for those you don't know. Showing concern requires rapport, being available and approachable to your partners, listening to them, and understanding their point of view.

Becoming a student of your partner's ministry is another way to demonstrate concern. Understanding their ministry as they understand it shows respect and appreciation for it. As you become familiar with your partners and they with you, uncertainty about your motives is partly dispelled. More importantly, you verify your concern for their well-being when you take actions that clearly show that you understand their interests.

But these are only the mechanics of demonstrating concern for others. Genuine concern comes from the heart. If we possess what Paul Hiebert describes as a biblical view of "Others," our concern will be authentic and attractive.[21] A biblical view of Others, Hiebert explains, begins with our common humanity with all people. This means that "At the deepest level of our identity as humans, there are no Others, there is only us" (Genesis 1:26; Psalm 148:11–13; Isaiah 45:22; Micah 4:1–2; Luke 10:25–37). If we are to have genuine concern for others it must be rooted in the belief that they are like us, made in the image of God, endowed with gifts, charged with responsibility, and free to stand or fall before God.

Hiebert continues, "In the church there are no Others; there are only us—members of the body of Christ" (Ephesians 4:4; Galatians 2:11–21; 3:28; 1 Corinthians 10–11; Acts 2:44; 4:32). Not only does this unity bridge the human distinctions of ethnicity, class, and gender, it binds us together as family. If we start with the view that our partners are our brothers and sisters in Christ, then our concern for their welfare will be matched by our concern for their dignity, freedom, and fellowship. Our concern will be adjusted by the reality that their welfare is bound up with our own.

Integrity in One's Words and Actions

Talk is cheap. If we hope to win others' confidence and build trust, our actions have to align with our words. Unlike faith, trust operates on what is seen—consistent and predictable behavior.

Trust requires integrity and consistency in one's words and actions. People whose actions match their beliefs are thought to have integrity, and thus to be worthy of trust. Inconsistency suggests that they may be dishonest and self-serving, and therefore untrustworthy.

Integrity, and the trust that derives from it, boil down to consistency in four basic areas:

Is what you know what you make known? If people believe we have been forthcoming with important information, honest about our feelings and views, they will begin to trust us. If they believe we have not shared all we should, they will become suspicious.

Full disclosure of information about the partnership is always preferred, but not always required. There are situations when you must keep a confidence or withhold information to avoid putting someone at risk. Even then you can give an explanation for not revealing the information.

You don't want people to feel that because of some hidden agenda you know more than you are saying. To avoid this trap, make your agenda known. Integrity requires openness about one's intentions and motives. Even when you are not sure what your agenda will be, it is better to say so than to leave your partner in the dark. Misinformation thrives in a vacuum.

Is there alignment between your words and actions? Consistency in words and actions is especially important in a partnership. Acting with integrity means keeping your promises.

Honest people may be tempted to gloss over this question. Any self-respecting person knows that it is dishonest to say one thing and do another. They would never intentionally behave that way. But that is not the problem. Inconsistencies between words and actions are not always intentional. In fact, it is the unintentional discrepancy that most often gets us into trouble. Ministry partners have to be very deliberate to follow through on both explicit and implicit commitments.

This is particularly challenging to global partnerships because of cultural and linguistic differences. What a Western visitor intends as a word of encouragement, for example, may be interpreted as a promise. Most people in the world express themselves indirectly. They are accustomed to reading between the lines of intentionally vague statements. Endorsement of a project can easily be taken as a pledge of support.

Next to strong cross-cultural communication skills, the best way to keep commitments in plain sight and mutually understood is by discovering shared vision, negotiating ground rules, and measuring results.

Is your behavior consistent across situations? Integrity requires that we share the same information with different people so that everyone has the same story. Trust grows when people know that you wouldn't change your position depending on the audience you are addressing or the situation in which you find yourself.

Is your behavior consistent over time? Integrity earns trust like an investment earns interest. It grows from small actions over time. An interesting thing about integrity is that while you may have lots of it, it usually takes a long time to prove it. This is because trust is based on what people see, not on what they hear. Actions have to support the words, not just once, but many times. As the evidence of integrity increases, trust increases.

To operate with integrity doesn't make one error-free and successful at all times. Most people don't expect perfection. They expect honesty. We can't always avoid mistakes or downturns that affect our partners. If you find you must break a promise, it is important to explain what happened and to assure them you are supportive and understand their disappointment. Such honesty goes a long way, not only to soften the blow, but also to assure them they can count on you to be up-front with bad news as well as good.

Achievement of the Results Promised to Others

There is more to trust than goodwill. Trust requires the achievement of results. That is to say, trust requires that those who depend on you actually get the results they expect from you. Others may be convinced you are looking after their interests, but they might not be convinced you have the skill, knowledge, or resources necessary to benefit their ministry. Trust requires that you deliver on your commitments.

Failure to deliver the results expected erodes the confidence others place in you. While ministry partners will typically be quite forgiving, extended time without results will never-the-less begin to erode trust. People enter into partnership with specific needs and expectations. If those needs go unsatisfied or under-satisfied for too long, you will be regarded as unworthy of trust—not because you are hard to get along with but because you don't have the ability to deliver.

The results I am referring to are not the big goals of the partnership. No, they are the many small things partners do to fulfill their responsibilities. While it is true that failure to achieve overall goals can erode trust, that is not how it usually happens. Partners who are unsuccessful in achieving their primary goals but who stay the course and follow through on the small commitments often gain an even stronger bond of trust.

In order to deliver the results expected of you, however, you must know what those expectations are. Trust requires clear, uncomplicated agreements about what each party will deliver in a given partnership. The surest paths to clear commitments are creating shared vision, developing ground rules, and measuring results.

In sum, everything in a partnership works both ways, especially with regard to trust. While this seems obvious, many people, when asked about the need to build trust, describe what others must do to demonstrate that they are worthy of trust. This is a counterproductive starting point. The assumption that others have to prove their trustworthiness is like saying they are guilty until proven innocent. A better starting point is to begin to trust, and, more importantly, show that you can be trusted.

Many ministry partnerships that fail do not fail for good reasons. They fail because of unrealistic expectations, self-serving agendas, excessive demands for accountability, or chronic inconsistencies between words and actions. Some partnerships fail for a lack of positive results, but if a partnership fails, it is usually because of distrust. By intentionally trusting first, demonstrating concern, acting with integrity, and achieving results, you can avoid or at least minimize distrust. Trust is not created overnight. It is the result of many small commitments made and kept.

Checklist Two

Managing the Relationship

Managing the relationship means asking tough questions and discussing the answers with your partner. Some of those questions include the following:

☐ Do we have a growing awareness of each other's interests and abilities?

☐ Can we say we have extensive formal and informal communications?

☐ Has it become easier to raise issues and resolve our differences?

☐ Does the alliance champion provide the coordination we need?

☐ Do we know where we are going with the partnership in the future?

☐ Has our direction changed since the partnership began, and is that change acceptable?

☐ Are we following the ground rules we set forth?

☐ Do we always consult one another before making key decisions that affect the partnership?

☐ Are we working to improve our relationship in ways other than work-related matters?

☐ Should the partnership be renegotiated? Should it be concluded?

Part Three: Results

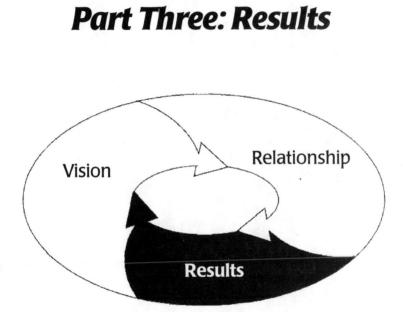

7
Meaningful Results

Partnership is not an end in itself. No, it exists to contend as one man for the faith of the gospel (Philippians 1:27). The decisive value of global partnership is that it creates results in the ministry of the gospel.

Partners who are not getting results are not really contending. More specifically, partners who are not getting *meaningful* results are not really contending. By definition every partnership gets some results, even if only some kind of effect on its surroundings. The question is, are they the right results? Do they reflect shared values? Do they mark progress toward a vision? Do they indicate faithfulness and obedience to God? Partners who understand and focus on meaningful results get the full potential benefits of partnership.

What Are Meaningful Results?

By *results* I mean the effects or outcomes produced by the joint effort of ministry partners. Results are the symbols of our labor and the footprints of our journey. Whether they are all, only part, or none of what we hoped to achieve, results do provide a point of comparison with our expectations. They tell us whether we are moving in the right direction and they let us know when we have arrived.

There are five criteria for assessing whether a partnership is producing meaningful results. These criteria determine how much partners will achieve through collaboration.

1. Meaningful results are **measured:** Partners know where they stand in relation to their vision because they constantly compare the present to the past, as well as to the plan and to the possibilities.

2. Meaningful results are **strategic:** they confirm the vision and values of the partnership.

3. Meaningful results are **balanced:** They benefit the partners in proportion to their contributions.

4. Meaningful results are **synergistic:** They are greater than either partner could have achieved alone.

5. Meaningful results are **co-created:** They come from joint learning and mutual change.

Measures for Assessing Progress

The first test of whether or not results are meaningful is this: Do you know what the results are? Certainly it is possible to produce good outcomes without knowing what they are. But as organizational structures go, partnerships are fragile. As we have seen, their strength relies heavily on shared values and proof that those values are being realized. Some of the evidence comes naturally through the quality of the relationship. But far more evidence comes through a deliberate effort to measure progress.

Measuring progress in a ministry partnership offers a number of benefits. In the first place, measuring provides evidence. Results mean very little if you don't know what they are. In the absence of clear measurements, just about anything can pass for success or failure. The process of measurement forces consequences out into the open. More importantly, there is a very good chance that different partners will measure outcomes differently unless they agree on what and how outcomes are to be measured.

A second benefit is that measurements give *feedback*. It is hard to correct your course unless you know where you are in relation to where you want to be. Measurements indicate what to stop doing, what to keep doing, and what to change.

Third, measurement enhances *motivation*. Few things motivate people more than to see their vision become a reality. Measurements also provide the opportunity to recognize people's contributions.

A fourth benefit of measuring progress is that measurements lead to *renewal*. The process of measuring results leads naturally to discussions about the vision, the relationship, and what constitutes meaningful results.

Finally, measurements give rise to *celebration*. A clear picture of progress gives occasion for praise and thanksgiving to God.

In its simplest form, a measurement is a comparison between two points. It might be a comparison between what exists and what is desired, or between what is happening today and the way things were in the past. By comparing the present to the past, or to an ideal, measurements mark passage from one condition to another. They indicate whether you are moving toward your vision or you need to make adjustments.

Measurements come in two basic kinds: quantitative and qualitative. Quantity is the amount of something; quality has to do with its essential nature. Quantitative measures refer to the use of numbers and statistics. Qualitative measures describe the character of something. Both types of measures are useful and necessary in ministry partnerships.

The easiest way to measure is to count things: the number of people confessing Christ, the number of people baptized, churches started, the number of students in a program, and so on. These are useful numbers to know, but their real value comes in comparison to other numbers. For example, the number of Christians compared to non-Christians in a community, the number of graduates compared to initial enrollments, or the number of churches today compared to the number ten years ago.

Some missiologists have argued that the most important outcomes cannot be reduced to numbers.[22] To be sure, the most important results in ministry are not tangible, and cannot be handled, counted, or ranked. How could you quantify spiritual progress? How can you measure faith, hope, or love with numbers? You can't, of course.

Fortunately, you don't have to quantify results to measure them. The essence of measurement is to make a comparison, not to count things. If the results you want are plainly quantifiable, go ahead and compare numbers. If not, compare qualities.

A qualitative measure is a descriptive comparison between the present and the ideal of a single attribute. It can also be a comparison between the present and the past with regard to an essential quality. For instance, suppose one aim of your partnership is to have healthy churches. In order to track progress you would first define the distinguishing attributes of a healthy church.[23] Provided such definitions are clear, mutually understood and affirmed, each attribute would provide a point of comparison with the present situation. Comparing what is happening today with each of the ideal attributes would constitute qualitative measurement of a healthy church.

Having visible measurements of progress is as vital and motivating to a partnership as it is to personal growth. It affects both the quality of the relationship and the direction of the alliance. Yet the measures themselves are meaningful only if there are clear expectations to begin with. Measurements have to be based on what partners seek to accomplish, their purpose, and their goals.

Without clear goals, measuring can find only, for example, that x number of new churches have been started, or that one church is different from another. The question of whether the churches are satisfactory cannot be answered without a point of reference. Clear goals make it possible to compare what is desired with what is actually happening.

Successful partners figure out what is meaningful to both organizations, then together find ways to measure progress. There is no simple formula for defining appropriate measurements— but neither is it rocket science. Setting up a measurement system takes time and effort. It is a skill partners must acquire and use repeatedly to ensure that the purpose of the partnership is achieved.

Proof of Strategic Impact

The second test of meaningful results is that they satisfy the underlying purpose of the partnership. Results are strategic when they show that the partnership is accomplishing what it set out to do. While there may also be, and often are, a number of unintended outcomes, strategic results reflect the core vision and values of the partnership. They are the end results in which, for example, evangelistic partnerships see new believers, church planting partnerships see new churches, economic development partnerships see improved living conditions, and so on. Strategic results answer the "So what?" question. Partners have to be able to see the fruit of their labor and say, "Yes, this is what it is all for. This is why we entered into partnership in the first place."

Balanced Returns on Investment

Genuine partnership consists of balanced results, not one-sided gains. Results are balanced when they meet or exceed each partner's expectations. Partners need to feel that what they are getting out of the partnership is at least equal to what they put into it. Ideally, results should be reciprocal so that both partners benefit substantially, making it a win-win situation. An imbalance can leave a partner feeling cheated or even exploited.

Obviously balance is good. And it should be easy to achieve. Unfortunately, it is not. Expectations of balance and fairness usually become noticeable only when they are violated. The challenge is as much a problem of perception as it is of reality. And perception of whether results are balanced is tied to both expectations and contributions. Each partner has certain expectations about what the partnership will accomplish. The more clearly these expectations are defined and negotiated, the more likely they will be perceived equally by both parties. Fuzzy or hidden expectations are almost certain to lead to different perceptions about the nature and outcomes of the relationship.

Even under the best of conditions expectations are difficult to manage. No matter how clearly they are defined at the beginning of a partnership, they tend to change over time. In most cases, the more successful the relationship, the more expectations become inflated. Unless changing expectations are periodically identified and renegotiated, results can appear out of line or inadequate. By contrast, you know you are getting balanced results when each partner feels it is getting enough from the partnership to keep going.

What a partner contributes to the relationship, or thinks it contributes, is the second factor in the perception of balance. Balance is a function of reciprocity and fairness. It is not a question of partners contributing an equal share. Rather, balance has to do with getting results that correspond to the level of contribution. A partner that contributes both funds and personnel will expect more than a partner that contributes only financially. A partner that contributes long-term financial support will expect more than a partner that provides one-time capital funds. The issue is not the amount a partner contributes but the perceived degree to which the results correspond to the level of contribution.

Therein lies a problem. Sometimes what a partner thinks it contributes may not correspond to what it actually contributes. Misperceptions usually occur for one of three reasons:

- Partners forget, or never knew, exactly what was contributed.

- Partners assume something was contributed that was not.

- Partners overestimate the real value of their contribution.

This last point is a common mistake, especially on the part of foreign donors. Unless they are aware of all of the costs, their investment can seem larger than it is. The result is often the perception that ministry outcomes don't match the level of contribution.

The answer to the problem of perception is both joint planning and record-keeping. Partners who continually plan together have the best chance of clarifying perceptions before they drift too far from reality. Keeping a record of contributions is also vitally important. Adequate records include not only financial transactions, but also records of time, key people, and technology.

Partners, however, need more than an inventory of contributions. They need a way to assess the value of those contributions. Thoughtful Christians agree that it is not self-serving to expect a good return on an investment (Matthew 25:14–30). The problem lies in how contributions are valued. Partners may place a different value on the same contribution. In some cultures, for example, the principal contribution and source of perceived benefit may be largely relational.[24] In such cultures, an expected benefit of a good relationship is loyalty. If a ministry does not achieve the planned outcomes, such as completing a project on schedule or fulfilling a matching grant, the relationship is seen to take precedence over due dates and dollar amounts. The funding partner, however, may value the time commitment more than the relationship and see the delay as a broken promise. Intercultural partners have to understand each other enough to appreciate how various contributions are valued.

The stability of a partnership is a function of the benefits the various parties find in it. Each partner must get significant results that are not only fair, but also that could not have been achieved alone.

Evidence of Synergy

It is universally understood that "Two are better than one, because they have a good return for their work" (Ecclesiastes 4:9 NIV). This is the underlying assumption of partnership. If partnership offers any advantage over going it alone, it is the possibility of creating synergy. Synergistic results are significant gains that neither partner could have achieved alone. They are that prized class of outcomes where the total effect is greater than the sum of its parts.

But synergy doesn't happen simply by partners deciding to cooperate. Synergy comes only from the strategic alignment of skills and resources to accomplish a specific objective. Partners who achieve synergy have three things going for them:

- knowledge of what it takes to accomplish a particular objective;

- understanding of each other's strengths and weaknesses;

- ability to leverage their strengths by combining strategic skills and resources.

In this way partners combine a wider set of different resources than either ministry would possess on its own.

Products of Joint Learning and Mutual Change

Results in partnership are most meaningful when they are co-created, the product of joint learning and mutual change. When partners are willing to learn and change together, they open up new, previously inaccessible possibilities.

While joint learning may occur in a number of ways, the most significant learning comes through tracking and analyzing ministry results. In contrast, unexamined results will almost certainly create blind spots that can lead to misperceptions as well as missed opportunities.

An unexamined result is like the unexamined life. It leaves you adrift in a sea of ambiguity, never certain of what your activities really mean. This can lead to apathy or a feeling that all is well while consuming great quantities of resources without making an appreciable difference in the advance of the gospel. Unexamined results can also lead to delusion, convincing yourself that the activity aligns with the espoused values. In fact, many ministries would be shocked to discover how much of what they say they believe does not actually line up with what they do. Unexamined results lead to failure. More often than not, failure occurs in ministry because learning has stopped, not because people don't believe in learning, but because they don't have adequate feedback about what is really going on.

Examining results is the feedback loop that enables learning and signals a need for change. It helps you realize the connection between what is really happening and what it actually means in the work of the gospel. Joint efforts to track and measure results can bring to light how present activities either serve or subvert the vision.

Whatever your measurements, defining substantive ways to "test the success" of the vision is in some ways a theological task. If nothing else, it leads you back to the significant questions.

- Is the kingdom of God advancing?

- Are God's people remaining faithful?

- Do we believe that God reigns?

When partners are willing to rethink the results of their efforts and make changes, they expand their capacity to produce meaningful results.

Success is Measured with God's Yardstick

However well-intended our goals or however precise our measurements, they are merely a clouded picture of God's assessment. In the end, the meaning of results is measured with God's yardstick. The tenuous differences between faithfulness and success or failure can be difficult to discern. During this process it is helpful to remember the words of J. I. Packer:

> After setting biblically appropriate goals, embracing biblically appropriate means of seeking to realize them, assessing as best we can where we have got to in pursuing them, and making any course corrections that our assessments suggest, the way of health and humility is for us to admit to ourselves that in the final analysis we do not and cannot know the measure of our success as God sees it.[25]

Those partners who focus on faithfulness over achievement are able to keep success in perspective. Faithfulness enables us even to fail if it will further God's purposes. So whether we succeed or fail, what matters is that we do it all for Christ, to exalt him, and to enjoy the rewards of serving God wholeheartedly.

8
Documentation

Partnership is all about managing expectations. The big challenge is the speed with which expectations change. This can either be because people forget or because they change their minds. Partners who are separated by great geographical or cultural distances are especially vulnerable to shifting expectations.

It is important to point out that change itself is not the problem. In fact, a partnership that is not altering expectations at some level is not really partnering. Global partners can expect to be in an almost constant state of negotiating perceptions, values, and expectations. That's why you need to put them in writing. Documentation provides an audit trail, a somewhat objective way to trace change over the passage of time. Unless partners take care to record essential agreements, transactions, and outcomes, they will not have the right information to evaluate progress.

Writing things down provides four important benefits:

- **History**—Documents and records collected over time tell a story. A contextually rich supply of data can yield valuable lessons.

- *Memory*—Without documentation it is easy to forget the facts you once knew. Written records are more likely to provide an accurate snapshot of the way things were, and an objective point of reference for resolving conflicts.

- *Currency*—Timely, informative data keeps everybody on the same page. When data is kept current, partners know where they are at any given time because they are working with the same information.

- *Measurement*—Appropriate records allow you to compare the present experience to past expectations. As pointed out in Chapter 7, the chief means to measuring results is comparison.

Some common types of documentation include project proposals, working agreements, financial reports, and project updates.

Project Proposals

A project proposal is the comprehensive planning document that spells out the parameters of a joint venture. This involves negotiating, or co-creating, the project with the partner in such a way that each has a clear picture of what is to be accomplished and how. It should include goals, timelines, costs, a list of who is responsible for what, and a description of materials, processes, and methodologies to be used. An outline of what should be included in a project proposal is provided in Figure 8.1.

Figure 8.1. Project Proposal Format

Project Proposal Format

- TITLE OF THE PROJECT

    Name of the ministry

    Address and contact information

- BACKGROUND

    What are the ministry's current activities?

    How did the need for the project arise?

    How does the project fit into the purpose/mission of the ministry?

- PURPOSE

    What do you want to achieve?

    What specific results are you seeking?

    What difference will it make in the work of the gospel?

- METHODOLOGY

    How do you plan to carry out the project?

    What major milestones must be accomplished to achieve desired results?

    What programs, activities, and techniques will you use to achieve the milestones?

- TIMELINE

    When will the project begin and end?

    What are the timelines to accomplish your milestones?

    What do you plan to accomplish by the end of 6 months? One year? Two years?

    If it involves stages, what are the stages and when do you expect to complete each?

- **Cost Estimates**

    What funds are needed for the entire project?

    Over what period of time are these costs projected?

    Where will you get the funds?

    How will the funds be used?

    How will the funds be accounted for?

- **Management**

    Who is responsible for each milestone or major part of the project?

    To whom should (name of organization) refer to resolve issues as they arise?

- **Required Inputs**

    In addition to funds, what other resources are needed?

    What human resources are needed to carry out the project?

    What special expertise or skill, if any, will be needed?

    What technical resources are needed to carry out the project?

- **Partner Inputs**

    What benefits do you expect from an alliance with (name of organization)?

    What specific contributions are you seeking from (name of organization): funds, personnel, technology, other?

    What is the amount of funds you will request, if any, from (name of organization)?

    When are the funds needed?

- **Expected Outputs**

    How will results be measured?

    What factors will indicate progress toward desired results?

What feedback mechanisms will be used to monitor progress?

What reports and updates will be required?

How often will progress be reviewed, yearly, quarterly, monthly?

- EVALUATION OF PROJECT

    How will the project be evaluated and by whom?

    How will (name of organization) participate in the evaluation process?

- AUTHORIZATION

    The prospective partner signs and dates the final version of the proposal.

    This includes two signatures: the ministry leader/director and normally a member of the board of directors, typically the chairperson.

Working Agreements

Working agreements are one way to capture expectations and freeze them in time for future reference. The working agreement is the foundational document that sets the partnership in motion. It is based on the needs and expectations defined in your partnership assessment, initial proposal, and ground rules.

Unfortunately some people do not like to use written agreements. Others resort to lengthy documents in an effort to guard against unforeseen events. On the one hand, it's important to clarify all essential expectations. On the other hand, no one wants a working agreement that looks like a mortgage contract.

The idea of a working agreement makes some ministry leaders uncomfortable. To them written agreements are impersonal and unnecessarily restrictive. They argue that oral contracts are friendly and give people their dignity by assuming that they are good for their word. However, if there is a disagreement, it becomes your word against theirs. You might think you agreed to one thing, but they claim you agreed to something else. Occasionally, people may lie to save face or get out of an obligation. More often they genuinely have a different understanding or memory of the oral agreement.

A working agreement does not have to look and feel like a legal contract. Very rarely do ministry partners need legal contracts. If you do, get advice from an attorney. You can determine whether or not a legal contract is necessary by answering one question: Would you ever take your partner to court for breach of contract?

International ministry partnerships are built and sustained on mutual trust and shared responsibility. For this reason, the primary purpose of the agreement is to establish general roles and responsibilities, not to police or coerce partners. Creating a legal document would offer no more benefits than those provided by a good working relationship. In fact, making the agreement a legal contract would undermine the spirit and purpose of the partnership. Legal authority presumes the ability to induce compliance by threat of punishment. Bringing legal action on a partner would give little benefit to the work of the gospel, and may be out of step with kingdom principles.

A cooperative structure such as I describe in this book is what holds a partnership together, not contracts and legal documents. This is especially true of an international network of ministries. The history of international ministry is full of struggles between foreign missions and local ministries that have come of age and are ready to take their place as equals in the work of the gospel.[26] Problems arise when the foreign mission insists on ownership of the local ministry. Legal contracts may ensure that the foreign mission retains possession of property, but it does nothing to ensure that the local ministry is biblically faithful and missionarily effective. That can only be achieved through cooperative structures. At the heart of any cooperative structure is the ability of the partners to maintain a unifying purpose, a trusting relationship, and a method to measure progress.

To develop an agreement that is both useful and friendly, work through the following three-step process, which culminates with the working agreement.

First, flesh out a *partnering proposition*. This is similar to a project proposal but without the fine points. It describes in brief what partners want from the relationship and what they can potentially bring to it. It is different from a project proposal in that it is necessarily broad-based and short on detail. It serves more as a platform for discussion than as a plan. The partnering proposition is the crucial first step on which to build the working agreement. The partnering proposition should answer the following questions as clearly and concisely as possible:

- What do you want to achieve?

- What specific results are you seeking?

- Who are you trying to help or reach out to? Where are they located? How many people could potentially be affected by this project?

- How do you plan to carry out the project?

- What major milestones must be accomplished?

- When will the project begin and end? If it involves stages, what are the stages and when do you expect to complete each one?

- What will the project cost? Over what period of time are these costs projected?

- What benefits do you expect from an alliance with (name of organization)?

- What role(s) do you expect (name of organization) to have? For example, providing funds, personnel, technology, and so forth.

- What amount of funds will you request, if any, from (name of organization)? When will the funds be needed?

Second, review and discuss *general principles and policies* for cooperation. Drafting an official statement of guidelines for cooperative work can facilitate this step. This is where you draw up ground rules as discussed in Chapter 3 and finalize the document. This would include general terms and conditions, such as what happens when the partner doesn't like your performance or changes the plan halfway through the project, or when you run into an unexpected obstacle. Important disclaimers should also be included, such as conditions under which you are not responsible for problems and delays. This document does not have to be signed, but it should be referred to in the working agreement. Partners International, for example, publishes a general set of guidelines for review and discussion in *Our Pledge to You* (See Partnership Resources: Two).

Third, prepare the *working agreement.* This may be either a standard form in which you fill in the blanks, or a customized letter of agreement. Either way the best agreements are short and uncomplicated. They should include:

- the name and description of the project, including estimated size and scope;

- reference to the partnering proposition (a copy should be attached);

- the schedule and deadline for completion ;

- the amount and schedule of funds/grants (how much money are you providing and when will the partner get it?);

- the number, roles, and reporting relationships of personnel (who will be working closely together);

- reference to the ground rules (principles and guidelines for cooperation).

It is assumed that both partners will have a chance to make changes before giving final approval.

A fourth step may be necessary for long-term or large-scale projects. An extensive project may be organized into discrete phases and a new agreement written for each phase. Details of a particularly complicated phase may also be included as an addendum.

Financial Reports

Financial reports typically include standard financial statements such as monthly "actual versus budget" reports, along with a record of "funds transfers" from one organization to the other. Annual financial reports include a "balance sheet," "statement of income and expenses," and a "statement of donations." Examples of these are available in Figures 8.2, 8.3 and 8.4. In partnerships involving large sums of money, audited financial statements are appropriate. Such audited statements may include a list of donations received from the partner organization.

Project Updates

Partnerships depend on the sharing of information. Project updates provide a standard format that helps to keep everyone informed of the current status. The project update is a regular report designed to clarify expectations, analyze how well those expectations are being met, and recommend steps for improvement. Unlike prayer letters and ministry reports that are written for external audiences, project updates are intended for internal use. They should provide a candid review of what has been accomplished since the last update, what has to be accomplished, and major constraints and concerns. Updates don't have to be long, but they do have to be descriptive as well as evaluative. In other words, well-written updates provide evidence of change as well as opinions about change. The best updates include pictures and possibly videos. Figure 8.5 depicts a standard project update.

Anyone entering into partnership should realize that expectations change. No written agreements, signed commitments, or guidelines for cooperation, however well-designed, will stop change from occurring. The best you can do is to manage change. Few things help more than access to relevant, timely, and explicit documentation.

Figure 8.2. Sample Balance Sheet

(Name of Recipient Ministry)

BALANCE SHEET
(Your fiscal year ending date)

ASSETS   National
                                                               Currency

Current Assets

Cash on Hand	1,800	
Cash in Bank	10,000	
Total Cash		11,800
Accounts Receivable		500
Cash Advance		1,000
Total Current Assets		13,300

Investments

Preferred Stock		2,000

Land, Property and Equipment

Land	20,000	
Building	40,000	
Transportation Equipment	7,000	
Office Equipment	2,000	
Furniture and Fixtures	2,000	
Total Fixed Assets	71,000	
Less: Accumulated Depreciation	28,000	
Total Land, Property and Equipment		43,000

Other Assets

Fixed Deposits		460

Total Assets | | 58,760

LIABILITIES and NET ASSETS

Current Liabilities

Accounts Payable	330	
Other Payables	1,984	

Total Liabilities | | 2,314

Net Assets (Please see Note below) | | 56,446

Total Liabilities and Net Assets | | 58,760

Note: The Net Assets amount is the difference between Total Assets and Total
Liabilities. The Net Assets figure comes from the Statement of Income
and Expenses.

Figure 8.3. Sample Statement of Income and Expense

(Name of Recipient Ministry)
STATEMENT OF INCOME AND EXPENSE
Year Ending (Date)

	National Currency	
Income		
Donations and Contributions (Note 1)	75,010	
Interest Income	590	
Other Income	100	
Total of All Income		75,700
Expenses		
Salaries and Wages	53,596	
Christmas Gifts	4,431	
Conference	2,972	
Insurance Premiums	2,467	
Depreciation	2,203	
Rent	1,868	
Transportation and Travel	761	
Light and Water	674	
Printing	551	
Repairs and Maintenance	528	
Communication	509	
General and Administrative	412	
Gifts, Donations and Contributions	331	
Office Supplies	260	
Promotional	259	
Taxes and Licenses	256	
Professional Fees	452	
Board/Executive Committee Meetings	149	
Board Allowance	125	
Total Expenses		72,804
Net Income		2,896
Beginning Net Assets (Prior year)		53,550
Ending Net Assets		56,446

Note: The Beginning Net Assets figure is from your prior year Balance Sheet. This Ending Net Assets figure is added to the Net Income figure for the current year (above) to arrive at the Ending Net Assets, which also appears on the Balance Sheet.)

Figure 8.4. Sample Statement of Donations

(Name of Recipient Ministry)

STATEMENT OF DONATIONS
Year Ending (Date)

Part 1

	National Currency
Churches - Local	10,250
Organizations - Local	11,100
Individuals - Local	2,000
(Name of Donor Ministry)	40,560
Others	11,100
TOTAL INCOME	75,010

Part 2

Date Funds Received	Check # (List each check)	U.S. Dollars	Other Currency	Exchange Rate	National Currency
Jan. 3	10010	1,000.00		2.37	2,370.00
Feb. 2	11002	600.00		2.55	1,530.00
Feb.15	11101	400.00		2.55	1,020.00
Mar. 4	11980	1,000.00		2.57	2,570.00
Apr. 3	12010	1,000.00		2.58	2,580.00
May 1	13100	1,200.00		2.43	2,916.00
May 5-Australia Special Project	665		888.00	1.81	1,607.28
Jun. 2	13998	1,200.00		2.48	2,976.00
Jul. 6	14551	1,200.00		2.48	2,976.00
Aug. 4	15116	1,200.00		2.48	2,976.00
Sep. 3	15898	1,272.00		2.47	3,141.84
Oct. 9	16010	1,550.00		2.48	3,844.00
Nov. 5	17001	1,432.00		2.49	3,565.68
Dec. 3	17896	1,693.46		2.51	4,250.59
Dec. 3-Canada	905		1,171.00	1.91	2,236.61
Total from (Donor Ministry name)		14,747.46	2,059.00		40,560.00

Figure 8.5. Project Status Report

PROJECT STATUS REPORT

_____   _____

Name of Individual Reporting   Date of Report

_____

Time Period Covered by this Report

Accomplished:

•

•

•

•

To Be Accomplished:

•

•

•

Constraints and Concerns:

•

•

•

_____

Signature

9
Learning and Change

Change is inevitable. Learning is not. Yet it is the ability to learn together that separates lasting partnerships from those that break apart at the first sign of adversity. Successful partnerships don't hold together because they cling to their original plans; they succeed because they learn and adjust to each other and to changing circumstances. Partnership at its best turns on joint learning and change.

Uncertainty and variability are always a part of partnership. In the early stages partners are more hopeful than clear about shared priorities. They may be even less certain about each other's ability to make good on their promises. As partners engage, relationships evolve in ways that are hard to predict. Over time, as partners get to know one another and the environment in which they are working, tasks define themselves. Partners not only have to learn *about* one another, they have to learn how to *collaborate with* one another. Even those who are highly experienced in the art of collaboration have to figure out how to work together in each new partnership.

Just about the time partners become comfortable with one another they discover that change has been at work from the start. Strategic priorities of the partners will shift independently of the partnership. Internal factors conspire to redirect priorities. External factors that partners cannot control produce change in the relationship. At various stages in the lifespan of the partnership, different needs arise. Contributions once vital to the relationship shift over time as the partnership achieves its goals. No matter how well-designed, partnerships remain vulnerable to all sorts of destabilizing factors.

In partnership, as in life, the way to cope with change and sometimes stay ahead of it is through learning. The ability to learn and adjust over time is imperative to effective partnering.

Three broad strategies to foster learning in ministry partnerships are described below.

Process Disciplines

Organizations employ a variety of processes depending on the nature of their work. Not all are required by all organizations. Some processes, however, are common to many types of organizations. Process disciplines are the most common and the most fundamental. A process discipline is one that must be performed routinely and effectively if the organization is to succeed.

Most ministry organizations, for example, have discovered the benefits of financial discipline. Financial planning, budgeting, and bookkeeping are standard practices. Since governing boards expect to have clear and accurate financial statements by which to assess the financial health of the organization, the need for the discipline of financial management is widely accepted. Unfortunately few organizations view learning and change as process disciplines that are as important to organizational effectiveness as financial performance.

Before process disciplines can be employed effectively, people have to see organizational life as a process rather than a structure. This involves looking not at lines of authority, but at the ways in which value is added to the processes that drive the organization—the priority setting process, the ministry outreach process, the fundraising process, the financial-management process, and the program evaluation process.

Successful partners don't solve problems by looking to structure. Instead, they look to processes that integrate people with the information, and the resources they need to do their work. That is one of the essential requirements of global partnership. People don't organize around jobs: They organize around what is to be accomplished.

An emphasis on process over structure means that partners should look horizontally across the partnership, from those who receive ministry to those who provide services and resources, including donors. It means involving people from different departments of the partnering organizations. It means gathering information about the flow of activities and outcomes across specialized departments. It means integrating processes across the partnership in order to better achieve desired ministry outcomes.

Organizations that wish to operate on a global level cannot afford to ignore process disciplines such as planning, feedback, and reflection. Together these processes constitute the engine of learning in ministry and in partnership.

Planning

Ministry leaders are quick to point out that the real value of planning is the process itself, rather than the end product. Plans are good but things do change. Strategies don't always work. Methods go out of date. People come and go, change their minds, or become distracted by more pressing concerns. Change makes written plans obsolete with amazing speed. On one hand, I can't think of a place where highly detailed plans are less useful than in the ministry of the gospel. On the other hand, few process disciplines are more important to ministry partnership than planning.

The power of planning is in the process, the discipline of collectively setting the focus, analyzing the forces that drive the ministry, and establishing milestones. When used as a collaborative learning experience, planning builds managerial skills, generates fresh information, identifies critical issues, improves communications, and reinforces the values of learning, innovation, and cooperation.

Plans alone have little value. What counts are results in the direction of a clear purpose. But for partners to establish and reestablish such a purpose and know results when they see them requires the collective thinking processes involved in planning. Thus the use of effective planning practices has a direct impact on the partnership's ability to learn and adjust.

Feedback

Without adequate information, planning is guesswork. Feedback about the processes and outcomes of ministry is the most important kind of information.

The three main approaches to gathering information are needs assessment, feedback mechanisms, and program evaluation. Needs assessment and program evaluation are processes that require special skills and special efforts beyond the scope of this book. Therefore the focus here is on process disciplines that fit within the scope of normal managerial responsibilities.

Feedback mechanisms are specific means by which vital information is captured and reported. That may sound fancy but it usually amounts to quarterly activity reports that include financial statements, reports on significant achievements, problems to be overcome, and action plans. Such reports are "feedback" insofar as they report back on the results of specific actions.

If you are clear about the vision and goals of the partnership, establishing feedback mechanisms is fairly straightforward. Once you decide how you will measure progress toward an objective, selecting a feedback mechanism is usually self-explanatory. For example, suppose the vision is to plant a church. Aubrey Malphurs, in his book *Planting Growing Churches*, suggests the stages include conception, development, birth, growth, maturity, and reproduction. Indicators or measures of progress in the conception stage include a clear understanding of core values, an overall church planting strategy, and initial implementation of the strategy. Corresponding feedback mechanisms would include a core values statement, a strategy statement, and monthly implementation review meetings.

Taken alone, feedback mechanisms reveal isolated events. But when accumulated over time, they reveal patterns. It is important to take the time to see emerging patterns rather than events in isolation. When you have two things to compare, you can see differences; when you have many, you begin to see patterns. The more of the big picture partners have, the more they can make connections and learn.

Reflection

We all know that learning requires more than the accumulation of knowledge. It is not enough to collect information; we must absorb it, internalize it, and connect it to concepts that we already understand. We must make it our own. It is when we have time to think about what we see and hear, to make patterns out of information, and to test ideas that we truly learn.

Putting reflection into the action of ministry is one of the most difficult disciplines to implement. Ministry people are typically action people who have little tolerance for what appears to be theoretical or academic. If the process of reflection doesn't appear to solve an immediate problem, it won't make it on to the agenda.

Reflection by a group of partners or team of leaders can take many forms. The best methods usually require a facilitator, someone who understands skillful discussion and how to use it. Peter Senge and colleagues describe a wide variety of techniques in *The Fifth Discipline Fieldbook*. However, it doesn't take outside facilitators to have productive moments of reflection. The key is to explore in depth without losing sight of the range of issues affecting the partnership. *The Partnership Self-Assessment,* reprinted in the back of this book, is designed to guide such a discussion (see Partnership Resources: Three). A good way to use this assessment is to schedule a full day for discussion at a quiet location away from the office. Significant reflection can also be achieved in the normal flow of work and managerial responsibilities. For example, you could have:

- Group and individual reflection times during the planning process.

- Informal small-group meetings where members are invited to speak candidly about their feelings and views.

- Retreats for prayer and spiritual renewal.

- Group and individual assignments that involve research and analysis.

- Personal performance appraisals, which can be a valuable one-on-one occasion to reflect on events and their meanings.

Partners who push at top speed and jump into new activities in rapid succession will never have the kind of environment in which learning can flourish. Unless partners have time to step back and learn from activities, they will never be able to evaluate whether they are moving in the right direction or just creating motion.

Employing process discipline means valuing the processes of collaborative inquiry, analysis, and decision-making. It means acquiring feedback from donors as well as the people you are trying to serve, from volunteers as well as staff, from service providers as well as board members. It means learning from what works and what doesn't work, and using that knowledge to shape the next cycle of planning.

Success at planning, feedback, and reflection require at the very least time to do it, practical tools for everyone to use, and a commitment on the part of senior management to work through the process from start to finish.

Positive Management Practices

Positive management practices, like process disciplines, enhance learning in partnerships. Typically, process disciplines foster learning at the group level while positive management practices improve individual learning.

In connection with their work, people mostly learn from experience. In fact, research indicates that adults do 90 percent of their learning from experience, rather than in schools or training programs.[27]

Unfortunately, most people view learning from experience as an almost subconscious activity. Workers and managers alike simply don't think about learning. It's something you do in school or training programs. At work it's a matter of solving problems, making decisions, and getting the job done. But the process of growth and improvement doesn't happen without learning.

The catch is that people learn for all kinds of reasons. There is no guarantee that individual learning will lead to organizational success. That's what makes learning the unseen force in organizational change. It is no less true in partnerships. The challenge to ministry leaders is to channel this energy in ways that benefit the organization as well as the individual.

Fortunately, ministry leaders don't need graduate degrees in education to enhance learning in work-life. What is necessary, however, is good management. A large portion of what managers do serves either to help or to hinder learning in the workplace. In some ways, positive management practices are equivalent to effective teaching and mentoring.

Ministry leaders can do a number of things to enhance learning from experience in organizational settings.

Establish an environment conducive to learning. By this I mean encouraging and valuing in your ministry the attitudes and practices of experimenting and adapting to new situations. This means increasing the acceptance of risk and recognizing the values of failure. It means seeking a greater accommodation to unconventional ideas. It means creating an enthusiasm for learning from experience within both individuals and groups. If you can build such a climate of values and expectations, you will have taken a great step toward not only enhancing learning but obtaining excellent results, as well.

Tell people what they need to do to succeed in their jobs. Don't let people struggle to figure out what is expected of them. Reassure them that they can do well in their jobs and tell them exactly what they must do to succeed.

Help people set achievable goals. Failure to achieve goals can disappoint and frustrate people. Encourage people to focus on their continued improvement, not just on their success or failure in specific tasks. Help them evaluate their progress by encouraging them to critique their own work, analyze their strengths, and work on their weaknesses.

Provide feedback on work performance and ministry outcomes. Take time to understand others well enough to give specific feedback aimed at helping them become more competent, satisfied individuals. One of most common situations for learning from experience occurs when individuals find that the approach they have been using, which made sense in the past, is no longer effective. Learning occurs when they reflect on the ineffectiveness of their approach, reinterpret the situation, then adopt a new approach.

Include people as active participants in decision-making. People take responsibility for decisions when they have contributed to identifying, analyzing, and solving the problem. Pose questions. Don't *tell* people something when you can *ask* them. Encourage people to suggest approaches to a problem and to anticipate the results.

Match individual talents to job requirements. Find out why people joined your organization, how they feel about their jobs, and what their expectations are. Then try to provide tasks and assignments that correspond to their interests and experiences. Explain how the work process and goals will help them achieve their own goals.

Make sure people have the information they need. Provide the information individuals and teams need to coordinate, manage, and evaluate their performance. This should include information about how the entire organization is performing so they can relate their part to the big picture. The more information shared across an organization, the more everyone learns.

Avoid stepping in and solving problems people should solve themselves. When you take over problems within the scope of other's responsibilities, you rob them of the chance to think for themselves. This is de-motivating and cuts learning short.

Celebrate success. Both positive and negative comments influence learning, but research consistently indicates that people are more affected by positive feedback and success. Praise builds self-confidence, competence, and self-esteem. Recognize sincere efforts even if the outcome is less than excellent. If a person's performance is weak, let that person know you believe he or she can improve and succeed.

Experienced leaders intuitively know that positive management practices are equivalent to effective training. The way people learn and improve in work-life is woven into the fabric of organizational life. Most people respond positively to clear expectations conveyed by an enthusiastic manager who shows a genuine interest in them. Good managers are those who respect us, listen to us, keep us informed, challenge us, and are genuinely interested in our personal success. All of this contributes to effective learning in the workplace. Of course, the opposite is also true. A lack of trust, opportunity, support, and feedback creates a poor learning environment.

Best Practices Research

Another way to foster learning that serves the organization as well as the individual is through observing and analyzing best practices. Research indicates that learning is most likely to occur when people have an opportunity to compare and contrast different approaches by different models. Capturing best practices is ideal because it involves looking at other ministries in order to discover basic principles that can be transferred to your own. Moreover, because the ministries studied are often in different settings and cultures, the findings are evaluated more objectively and adopted with less defensive reactions.

Observing others often affords us the opportunity to abandon our preconceived notions. Vicarious learning allows freedom to think in more original, innovative ways. Because we are not held responsible for ideas observed in others, we feel freer to invent and create.

One example of capturing best practices is the Learning Exchange program sponsored by Partners International. Each year a series of meetings are held in different regions of the world in which Two-Thirds world missions exchange stories and best practices of how indigenous Christian communities emerge and grow. Not only are ministry leaders learning new ideas for their own ministries, they are learning to capture their own best practices to share with others.

Sharing best practices is a refreshing way for ministries to learn from each other, and thus improve their partnerships as well as their own organizational effectiveness.

A Partnership in Action

Richard Makuyane now has an official ministry—Hope for Southern Africa (HSA)—based in Mabopane, South Africa. Through a strategy of evangelistic tent meetings followed by long-term discipleship of new believers, home groups are organized into small churches. Because HSA works in slums and impoverished communities, literacy programs and self-help projects are an integral part of the discipleship and church growth.

But Richard is a man without training, himself barely able to read. He knows little of financial dealings and recording data and management. In 1980, Allen Lutz, then vice president of Partners International, arrived on the scene. It was immediately apparent to him that the local churches, though determinedly self-sustaining, were too small and too poor to carry the bigger ministry of HSA. A partnership was formed between the two that produced kingdom benefits far beyond what either could have done alone.

It may sometimes appear that a good relationship is all partners need in order to succeed, or that partners who treat each other with dignity and share information freely can surely make a partnership work. But a closer look will reveal that partners who work well together are also learning together. They may not always be aware of it, but they are aware of having a sense of adventure. Together they take risks, help each other set and meet goals, obtain constant feedback about ministry activities, and take time out to reflect and pray together. When things go wrong, they seek solutions together and search for new ideas and fresh insight within and outside of the ministry. Clarifying expectations, setting goals, talking about them frequently, and examining ministry outcomes are all part of what successful ministry allies routinely do.

Richard Makuyane understands this.

> Preaching the gospel and discipling Christians is something I do well, but management and financial matters are not my strong points. If it were not for Gisela Nicholson's constant help with accounting, reporting, and communicating, this partnership would not be alive.

Gisela is a German immigrant to South Africa and the primary link between the two partners. Through Gisela, not only has HSA been served in unexpected ways, but Partners International has gained a better understanding of the role of an alliance champion.

"Money for projects is important," Richard says, "but a relationship is more than giving and receiving money. We need you to come and work with us. Add your gifts and talents to ours. Then I go out and set up my tent, and I preach the gospel."

Checklist Three

Measuring Results

Measuring the results of the partnership means tracking and evaluating the tangible outcomes. Periodically schedule a review with your partner and discuss the following questions:

☐ Do we have a clear picture of the goals we have achieved at this point?

☐ Are we achieving the results we intended?

☐ Are we measuring real impact or merely activities?

☐ Have our goals proven to be the kind that we can really make happen?

☐ Are the documentation methods adequate? Are we capturing the kind of information that is vital to the partnership?

☐ Are we making good use of process disciplines such as planning, feedback, and reflection?

☐ Have we fostered an environment in which learning is valued and carried out?

☐ Do we know what to do better to meet our goals between now and the next review?

☐ Can we honestly say we each have a sense of joy in the journey? When was the last time we celebrated our relationship?

☐ Are we each getting the benefits we need from this relationship?

Resource One:
Partner Assessment and Selection

Selecting a partner involves a fair amount of research. There is much that one can easily overlook or forget. The following checklist will remind you of important questions, and help guide the process.

It may not be necessary to answer all of the questions in every situation, and there may be other questions to add. The advantage of a checklist is that it is elastic. You can expand or collapse it based on the situation.

	Current Status			Action (When & Whom)
	Have it	Don't have it	Needs work	
Identify Target Group				
Who is to be served by the ministry?				
What needs are to be met?				
What is the situation of the larger Christian community?				
What needs assessment research is available or needed?				

	Current Status			Action (When & Whom)
	Have it	Don't have it	Needs work	
Define Program				
What is the ministry's strategic vision?				
What are the ministry's goals and objectives?				
What is their approach to ministry?				
How effective has the ministry been?				
What are the credentials and experience of the leaders?				
What does the ministry do well? What are its strengths?				
What does the ministry do poorly? What are its weaknesses?				
Describe Partner Organization				
How is the ministry structured?				
What is its official/legal status?				
What are its basic policies?				
Who are the board of directors and what roles do they fill?				
What relationship does the ministry have with other organizations and churches?				

	Current Status			Action (When & Whom)
	Have it	Don't have it	Needs work	
What means of accountability does the ministry demonstrate?				
Determine Financial Status				
What financial records are available to assess past performance?				
What ability does the ministry have to provide financial reports?				
What are the sources of income?				
What percentage of income is from foreign sources?				
What changes would occur if projected income is not met?				
What extent of access does the ministry have to outside sources of assistance?				
Profile the History				
What events brought the ministry into existence?				
Who were the founding leaders?				
What was the original vision?				

| | Current Status | | | Action (When & Whom) |
	Have it	Don't have it	Needs work	
What are the important milestones in the ministry's history?				
Determine Value Fit				
What are the ministry's tenets of faith?				
What is the philosophy of ministry?				
How do their actions demonstrate their beliefs?				
How does the ministry's strategic vision fit with our priorities?				
Identify Desired Outcomes				
What does the ministry expect of us?				
What can we reasonably expect to achieve?				
What will happen if we do not get involved?				
Consider Alternatives				
Should a different ministry reach out to the target group?				
Should a different organization collaborate with this ministry?				
What strategic alliances could benefit the ministry?				

	Current Status			Action (When & Whom)
	Have it	Don't have it	Needs work	
What capability do we have to serve the ministry?				
What other proposed programs might take priority over this program?				
Assess Overall Situation				
What are the external opportunities and threats?				
What are the internal strengths and limitations?				

Resource Two:
Our Pledge to You

Introduction

Partners International is committed to creating and growing communities of Christian witness in partnership with God's people in the least Christian regions of the world. Central to this commitment is the pledge to collaborate with non-Western indigenous missions.

This booklet represents the fundamental commitments between Partners International and its mission partners. While the statements do not constitute a comprehensive agreement, they represent the core values and actions critical to building and sustaining a viable partnership.

Common Ground

The first task of any partnership is to establish common ground. If you can rejoice in the following statements and affirm them with us, we have common ground on which to build a partnership in the gospel.

As those who share in God's grace with each other (Philippians 1:7), who have been qualified to share in the inheritance of the saints in the Kingdom of light (Colossians 1:12), who share in the heavenly calling (Hebrews 3:1), who share in His holiness (Hebrews 12:10), and who will share in the glory to be revealed (1 Peter 5:1), the following principals will govern our working relationship:

1. We are called to invest our lives and resources in Christ's ministry of reconciliation (2 Corinthians 5:18).

2. God has given His church a variety of gifts to complement each other in the ministry of equipping it to fulfill its mandate for the glory of Christ (Ephesians 4:11–13).

3. In seeking to fulfill this mandate, we recognize that our enablement does not depend on human criteria such as wealth, education, experience, and so on, but on the Holy Spirit (Zechariah 4:6).

4. It is both an honor and an obligation for Christians to assist one another in the work of Christ (2 Corinthians 8:1–15).

5. Any God-honoring service should be carried out in a spirit of mutual respect, trust and submission in the Lord (Colossians 3:23–24; Galatians 5:13).

6. Mutual accountability is an integral aspect of Christian stewardship (1 Corinthians 4:2; Romans 14:12).

7. Our motivation should be that of a servant in keeping with the example of Christ (Philippians 2:1–11).

Mutual Expectations

There are some things all partners in the gospel should expect from one another. In general, partners must be able to count on one another to:

1. Establish written plans that clearly define the goals and action steps of the joint project. Such plans are developed in a collaborative, open manner and subject to revision at any time.

2. Give consistent and thoughtful attention to the goals of the joint project and to consider themselves mutually accountable for the relative success or failure of the goals and the relationship.

3. Provide appropriate and sufficient resources and attention to the joint project in order to maximize its chances of success, growth, and faithfulness to God.

4. Persist in sharing information freely and in an undistorted manner.

5. Review and reflect on the operations of the joint project to ensure that it is moving toward appropriate goals and fulfilling mutual aspirations.

6. Identify and confront all disagreements and conflicts immediately and to devote substantial time, resources, and personal effort to the resolution or management of all conflicts, on behalf of the project's fulfillment.

7. Maintain the theological position put forth in their Statement of Faith and to inform one another of any significant changes in position.

8. Expect the unexpected. In a rapidly changing world, it is impossible to anticipate and plan for every opportunity or problem that might present itself. Therefore, partners ought to be able to count on each other to remain flexible and willing to share risk.

Our Commitment

There are some things unique to each partnership. With God's help you can count on us to:

1. Appoint a representative to oversee all aspects of Partners International's involvement in the joint project. In most cases this is an Area Director who manages other partnering relationships in the region.

2. Promote the joint project by: (a) reporting on the project in newsletters and other forms of media; (b) presenting the joint project to individuals, small groups, and church missions committees.

3. Fund an appropriate portion of the joint project by: (a) working closely with you to define specific projects that can be presented to funding sources; (b) appealing to individuals, churches, and foundations for charitable contributions; (c) giving block grants which provide a target for fund raising and a timetable for budgeting purposes.

4. Maintain separate accounts so that it is clear how much has been given by donors for the joint project.

5. Transfer funds through a method mutually agreed upon with the approval of your governing board, and in ways that are consistent with the intention of the donors.

6. Disburse funds only on the basis of mutually approved projects. Such funds are intended to help achieve the project goals and temporary in duration.

7. Fund joint projects in such a way that the funds stimulate or stabilize the self-reliance of our mission partners.

8. Meet all obligations with the understanding that financial support is conditioned by the charitable giving of God's people. A Partners International grant is a goodwill promise made by faith.

9. Safeguard the lives of ministry workers and the ministry as a whole in situations where Christians are put at risk by religious or political prejudice. This includes establishing security guidelines and following them.

10. Work cooperatively while remaining organizationally independent. We will not interfere in the administration of your organization, but encourage you to follow God's guidance, as you understand it.

11. Periodically assess the partnership by these criteria. We recognize that things change, including partnerships themselves.

In addition, new prospective partners can count on us to:

1. Engage only in joint projects the focus and direction of which coincide with our mandate to create and grow communities of Christian witness in the least Christian regions of the world.

2. Assess a ministry's partnership readiness before developing action plans and committing people and resources to a collaborative effort.

3. Seek the counsel of other Christian leaders in the area before agreeing to a joint project.

4. Determine not only where a ministry is today but envision where it could be as part of a joint project with Partners International.

5. Refuse alliances with ministries that have significantly different theological positions or philosophy of ministry.

Our Expectations

There are some particular things we expect from you. We depend on you to:

1. Make every effort to live up to the eight mutual expectations listed above.

2. Relate officially to Partners International through a governing board of directors, a board that is informed, involved, and ultimately responsible for the joint project.

3. Appoint a representative to oversee all aspects of your involvement in the joint project. In most cases this will be the ministry director. In large organizations it may be a member of the leadership team.

4. Provide a minimum of three reports per year, due January, May, and September, updating the status and progress of joint projects. Additional updates may be required in some cases.

5. When ministry leaders are enrolled in Partners International's sponsorship program, provide information including but not limited to (a) personal data on a standard form and a written, personal testimony, (b) a close-up color photo and negative of the worker and spouse, (c) and three prayer letters per year, due in January, May, and September.

6. Submit new projects and changes to existing projects through the Project Proposal Form, and thereby avoid obligating Partners International to any project without previous written agreement.

7. Inform us in advance of any plans to promote your ministry or the joint project in the USA or any country where Partners International associated councils are located. This includes Australia, Canada, Japan, New Zealand, South Africa, and the United Kingdom.

8. Provide an audited financial statement by the fourth month after the close of your fiscal year. Where total funds sent by Partners International meet or exceed US $20,000 in the fiscal year, an independent, CPA equivalent auditor must prepare the audit. Such audited statements must include a list of donations received from Partners International that agrees with the income and expense statement. Partners International will provide an example of what is expected in the financial statements.

9. Make available, after reasonable notice, additional financial records for Partners International's internal financial reviews, which may occur not more than once in two years.

Our Statement of Faith

We Believe . . .

- We believe in the Holy Scriptures as originally given by God, divinely inspired, infallible, entirely trustworthy; and the supreme authority in all matters of faith and conduct. . .

- One God eternally existent in three persons, Father, Son, and Holy Spirit. . .

- Our Lord Jesus Christ, God manifested in the flesh, His virgin birth, His sinless life, His divine miracles, His vicarious and atoning death, His bodily resurrection, His ascension, His mediatorial work, and His personal returning power and glory. . .

- The salvation of lost and sinful man through the shed blood of the Lord Jesus Christ by faith apart from works, and regeneration by the Holy Spirit. . .

- The Holy Spirit, by whose indwelling the believer is enables to live a holy life, to witness and work for the Lord Jesus Christ. . .

- The unity of the Spirit of all true believers, the Church, the Body of Christ. . .

- The resurrection of both the saved and the lost; they that are saved unto the resurrection of life, they that are lost unto the resurrection of damnation.

This statement of faith is identical to that of the World Evangelical Alliance.

Our Prayer

The Servant Song[28]

Brother let me be your servant,
Let me be as Christ to you.
Pray that I might have the grace
to let you be my servant too.

We are pilgrims on a journey,
We are brothers on the road.
We are here to help each other
walk the mile and bear the load.

I will weep when you are weeping,
When you laugh, I'll laugh with you.
I will share your joy and sorrow
till we've seen this journey through.

When we sing to God in heaven,
We shall find such harmony,
Born of all we've known together
of Christ's love and agony.

Brother let me be your servant,
Let me be as Christ to you.
Pray that I might have the grace
to let you be my servant too.

Resource Three: Partnership Self-Assessment

Partnership Self-Assessment is a personal approach to partnership evaluation. The idea is to have both individual and group scores so that partners can celebrate the high scores and discuss how to improve the low scores. First, distribute copies of the Self-Assessment to each of the alliance team members from both organizations. Have them complete the Self-Assessment individually so that everyone has his or her own score. Second, combine the scores of all team members in each partner organization so that you have two completed Self-Assessments, one for each partner organization. Finally, discuss the results and what steps might be taken to further develop the partnership.

For each statement, check "rarely," "sometimes," or "often" to describe how consistently you and your partners have the described experience.

	Rarely	Some times	Often
1. I have a clear sense of what the partnership is intended to accomplish.			
2. I can explain clearly the gap we fill in one another's ministry.			
3. My ministry is definitely getting the benefits it needs from this relationship.			
4. We have clear mutual expectations about how to work together.			
5. I know what is expected of me in this relationship.			
6. Our partnership problems get resolved quickly.			
7. It is easy to work together.			
8. Partners respond quickly to my concerns and issues.			
9. We follow the ground rules fairly closely.			
10. We make compromises to reach our shared goals.			
11. I work to develop our relationship separate from ministry activities.			
12. I have a clear awareness of our partner's interests and abilities.			
13. We consult one another before making key decisions that affect the partnership.			

	Rarely	Some times	Often
14. We explore new opportunities together.			
15. We are achieving the results we intended.			
16. We are measuring real impact and not merely activities.			
17. I understand where we are going with the partnership in the future.			
18. I know what to do better to meet our goals.			
19. I have a sense of joy in the journey.			
20. We pray and worship together.			

Scoring. Score the self-assessment test using the following instructions:

- Assign five points for each statement marked "often."

- Assign three points for each statement marked "sometimes."

- Assign one point for each statement marked "rarely."

In general, an overall score of 75 represents a satisfactory level of partnership effectiveness, 85 represents a good level, and 95 or higher represents an exceptional partnership experience.

The Author

Daniel Rickett is Assistant Professor of Leadership in the School of International Leadership and Development at Eastern University, St. Davids, Pennsylvania, and Senior Advisor of Partnership Development and Strategy for Partners International, Spokane, Washington, USA. In addition to teaching, Daniel provides consultation and specialized services to Two-Thirds world missions. He has conducted program evaluations, facilitated intercultural partnerships, and guided organizational capacity building for over twenty-five years. He has served on the board of directors of six non-profit ministries in the USA, five of which he helped to create. Daniel is a graduate of Michigan State University (Ph.D., Adult and Continuing Education) and Wheaton College Graduate School through Daystar University (M.A., Intercultural Communications).

Daniel is the author of *Building Strategic Relationships* (2000), co-editor of *Supporting Indigenous Ministries*, a Billy Graham Center Monograph (1997), and co-author with his wife, Michele, of *Ordinary Women: Developing a Faithwalk Worth Passing On* (2001).

Endnotes

1. Gordon Aeschliman, *Global Trends: Ten Changes Affecting Christians Everywhere* (Downers Grove, IL: InterVarsity Press, 1990), 190.

2. http://www.ad2000.org/status.htm.

3. Andrew Walls, *The Missionary Movement in Christian History* (Maryknoll: Orbis, 1996).

4. Larry D. Pate, *From Every People: A Handbook of Two-Thirds World Missions with Directory/Histories/Analysis.* (Monrovia, CA: MARC, 1989), 16–17.

5. Charles Van Engen, in *Supporting Indigenous Ministries* by Daniel Rickett and Dotsey Welliver, eds. (Wheaton, IL: Billy Graham Center, Wheaton College, 1997), vii.

6. In *Their Blood Cries Out,* Paul Marshall with Lela Gilbert documents that in more than 60 countries worldwide, Christians are harassed, abused, arrested, tortured or executed specifically because of their faith. David Barrett suggests that the average rate of martyrdom is about 160,000 Christians per year. David B. Barrett, George T. Kurian, and Todd M. Johnson, eds. *World Christian Encyclopedia: A Comparative Survey of Churches and Religions in the Modern World,* Volume 1 (New York, NY: Oxford University Press, 2001), 11.

7. See James H. Kraakevik and Dotsey Welliver, eds., *Partners in the Gospel: The Strategic Role of Partnership in World Evangelization* (Wheaton, IL: The Billy Graham Center, 1991). Also William D. Taylor, ed., *Kingdom Partnerships for Synergy in Missions* (South Pasadena, CA: William Carey Library, World Evangelical Fellowship Missions Commission, 1994). And Daniel Rickett and Dotsey Welliver, eds., *Supporting Indigenous Ministries* (Wheaton, IL: The Billy Graham Center, 1997).

8. Phill Butler, "Why Strategic Partnerships? A Look at New Strategies for Evangelism," in *Partners in the Gospel: The Strategic Role of Partnership in World Evangelization,* James H. Kraakevik and Dotsey Welliver, eds. (Wheaton, IL: The Billy Graham Center, 1991), 27–40.

9. Daniel Rickett, *Building Strategic Relationships: A Practical Guide to Partnering with Non-Western Missions* (San Jose, CA: Partners International, 2000).

10. World Evangelical Alliance (formerly World Evangelical Fellowship), http://www.worldevangelical.org/default.htm.

11. The full text of the *Lausanne Covenant* is available in the official compendium of the Congress, *Let the Earth Hear His Voice* (Minneapolis, MN: World Wide Publications, 1974). It is also available in *Lausanne Occasional Papers, No. 3, The Lausanne Covenant—An Exposition and Commentary* by John Stott (Wheaton, IL: Lausanne Committee for World Evangelization, 1975).

12. "The Gospel of Jesus Christ: An Evangelical Celebration" was composed by the Committee on Evangelical Unity in the Gospel, P.O. Box 5551, Glendale Heights, IL 60139–5551. Copies are available by writing to Christianity Today Reprints, 465 Gunderson Drive, Carol Stream, IL 60188, or by e-mail to CTEditor@aol.com.

13. Charles R. Taber, "Structures and Strategies for Interdependence in World Mission," *Mission Focus: Current Issues,* edited by Wilbert R. Shenk (Scottdale, PA: Herald Press, 1980). 453–78.

14. Duane Elmer, *Cross-Cultural Conflict: Building Relationships for Effective Ministry* (Downers Grove, IL: InterVarsity Press, 1993) 178–180.

15. Anglo-American refers to the cultural influence of the British and northern European ancestors. Although Anglo-American culture still dominates the United States it helps to distinguish it from others such as African American, Chinese American, and Latin American cul-

tures. The United States is a stew of over 280,000,000 people whose ancestors came from nearly every country in the world. This mix makes it difficult to speak of "American culture" with any consistency.

16. "The Willowbank Report—Gospel and Culture," *Lausanne Occasional Papers No. 2* (Wheaton, IL: Lausanne Committee for World Evangelization, 1978), 7.

17. John Stott, "The Lausanne Covenant—An Exposition and Commentary," *Lausanne Occasional Papers No. 3* (Wheaton, IL: Lausanne Committee for World Evangelization, 1975), 25.

18. Donald K. Smith, *Creating Understanding* (Grand Rapids, MI: Zondervan Publishing House, 1992), 251–266.

19. Ibid., 257.

20. William Bergquist, Juli Betwee, and David Meuel. *Building Strategic Relationships: How to Extend Your Organization's Reach Through Partnerships, Alliances, and Joint Ventures* (San Francisco, CA: Jossey-Bass Publishers, 1995).

21. Paul G. Hiebert, "Critical Issues in the Social Sciences and Their Implications for Mission Studies," *Missiology: An International Review* (24, No. 1, January 1996): 77–80.

22. Samuel Escobar, "Evangelical Missiology: Peering into the Future from a Critical Historical Moment." Paper presented at the World Evangelical Fellowship Missions Commission Missiological Consultation, Iguassu, Brazil, October, 1999.

23. See the "Eight Quality Characteristics" of healthy churches in Christian A. Schwarz's, *Natural Church Development* (Carol Stream, IL: ChurchSmart Resources, 1996).

24. Patrick Sookhdeo, "Cultural Issues in Partnership in Mission," in W. D. Taylor (ed.), *Kingdom Partnerships for Synergy in Missions* (South Pasadena, CA: William Carey Library, World Evangelical Fellowship Missions Commission, 1994), 49–66.

25. J. I. Packer, *A Passion for Faithfulness: Wisdom from the Book of Nehemiah* (Wheaton, IL: Crossway Books, 1995), 209.

26. For background on the question of moratorium and church/mission tensions, see James A. Scherer: 1964; Vergil Gerber (ed.): 1971; C. Peter Wagner: 1972; Gerald H. Anderson and Thomas F. Stransky: 1976; Pius Wakatama: 1976; Johannes Verkuyl: 1978; W. Harold Fuller: 1980.

27. Victoria J. Marsick, ed., *Learning in the Workplace* (New York, NY: Croom Helm, 1987).

28. The Servant Song by Richard Gillard. 1977 Scripture In Song (a div. of Integrity Music, Inc.)/ASCAP All rights reserved. Used By Permission. Int'l Copyright Secured.

Further Reading

Allen, R. *Missionary Methods: St. Paul's or Ours?* Grand Rapids, MI: Eerdmans Publishing, 1962.

————. *The Spontaneous Expansion of the Church.* Grand Rapids, MI: Eerdmans Publishing, 1962.

Anderson, G. H. and Stransky, F., eds.
Mission Trends No. 1. Grand Rapids, MI: Eerdmans, 1974
Mission Trends No. 2. Grand Rapids, MI: Eerdmans, 1976

Arias, M. "Mutual Responsibility." *IRM* 60 (1971): 249–258.

Aryeetey, S. "From Paternalism to Partnership." *EMQ* 31 (1995): 58.

Ayivi, E. "Joint Apostolic Action in Dahomey." *IRM* 61 (1972): 144–149.

Baba, P. "Nigerian Missionaries Sent Out of Africa." *Pulse* 24 (November 24, 1989): 5.

————. "We Need to Work Together to Develop Good Relationships." *EMQ* 26, no. 2 (April, 1990): 131–133.

Barrett, D. B., Kurian, George T. and Johnson, Todd M. eds. *World Christian Encyclopedia: A Comparative Survey of Churches and Religions in the Modern World,* Volume 1, New York, NY: Oxford University Press, 2001.

Bates, G. E. "A Study of the Processes of Conflict Resolution Between a Protestant Mission and Selected National Churches Overseas." Ph.D. dissertation, Michigan State University, 1975.

Bauer, P. T. *Equality, the Third World, and Economic Delusion,* 1981.

Bayne, S. F. Jr., ed. *Mutual Responsibility and Interdependence in the Body of Christ: with Related Background Documents.* New York, NY: Seabury Press, n.d.

Beaver, R. P., ed. *The Gospel and Frontier Peoples: A Report of a Consultation December 1972.* South Pasadena, CA: William Carey Library, 1973.

————. *To Advance the Gospel: Selections from the Writings of Rufus Anderson.* Grand Rapids, MI: Eerdmans Publishing, 1967.

Bell, C. R. and Shea, Heather. *Dance Lessons: Six Steps to Great Partnerships in Business and Life.* San Francisco, CA: Berrett-Koehler Publishers, 1998.

Bennett, C. "Welcome to Missions' Third Era." *Mission Today* 96 (1996): 107–110.

————. *God in the Corners: Personal Encounters Discovering God's Fingerprints in Remote Corners of our World.* San Jose, CA: Partners International, 1997.

Bergquist, J. A. and Manickam, P. K. *The Crisis of Dependency in Third World Ministries.* Madras: Christian Literature Society, 1974.

Bergquist, W., Betwee, J. and Meuel, D. *Building Strategic Relationships: How to Extend Your Organization's Reach Through Partnerships, Alliances, and Joint Ventures.* San Francisco, CA: Jossey-Bass Publishers, 1995.

Beyerhaus, P. "The Three Selves Formula: Is It Built on Biblical Foundations?" *IRM* 53 (October 1964): 393–407.

————. and Lefever, H. *The Responsible Church and the Foreign Mission*. Grand Rapids, MI: Eerdmans Publishing, 1964.

Blomberg, C. L. *Neither Poverty Nor Riches: A Biblical Theology of Material Possessions*, Grand Rapids, MI: Eerdmans, 1999.

Boer, J. H. "Missions: Heralds of Capitalism or Christ?" Ibadan, Nigeria: Daystar, 1984.

Bonk, J. J. *Missions and Money: Affluence as a Western Missionary Problem*, Maryknoll: Orbis Books, 1991.

————. "Paying National Pastors." *EMQ* 34 (October 1998): 392–3.

Bosch, D. J. *Transforming Mission: Paradigm Shifts in Theology of Mission*. Marknoll, NY: Orbis Books, 1991.

————. "Towards True Mutuality: Exchanging the Same Commodities or Supplementing Each Others' Needs?" *Missiology* 6, no. 3 (July 1978): 283–296.

Bowers, J. "Sending and Receiving in the Light of Equal Partnerships in Mission." *EMQ* 33 (1997): 186–194.

Braaten, C. E. "The Triune God: The Source and Model of Christian Unity and Mission." *Missiology* 18, no 4 (October 1990): 415–427.

Buhlmann, W. *The Coming of the Third Church*. Translated by S. J. Woodhall and A. N. Other. Maryknoll: Orbis Books, 1978.

Butler, P. "Why Strategic Partnerships? A Look at New Strategies for Evangelism." In J. H. Kraakevik and D. Welliver, eds., *Partners in the Gospel*, Wheaton, IL: Billy Graham Center, 1993.

————. "Why Partner?" *Mobilizer* 7 (1996): 1–8.

————. "Strategic Partnerships: Sixteen Key Effectiveness Principles." *Missions Frontiers* 19 (May/June 1997): 34–5.

Bush, L. *Funding Third World Missions: the Pursuit of True Christian Partnership*. Singapore/Wheaton, IL: World Evangelical Fellowship Missions Commission, 1990.

————. and Lutz, L, *Partnering in Ministry: The Direction of World Evangelism*. Downers Grove, IL: Inter Varsity Press, 1990.

Castillo, M. "Harnessing Filipino Missionary Potential—A New Movement Picks Up Steam." *Pulse* 25 (August 24, 1990): 5.

Chandler, P. G., *God's Global Mosaic: What We Can Learn from Christians Around the World*. Downers Grove, IL: InterVarsity Press, 2000.

Chiang, Samuel E. "Partnership at the Crossroads: Red, Yellow, or Green Light?" *EMQ* 28 (July 1992): 284–289.

Chinchen, D. "The Patron-Client System: A Model of Indigenous Discipleship." *EMQ* 31 (October 1995): 446–451.

Cho, D. "Korean Missions Built on Sacrifice." *Pulse* 25 (May 11, 1990): 5.

Clark, D. E. "Receiving Churches and Missions." *EMQ* 7 (1971): 201–210.

————. *The Third World and Mission*. Waco, TX: Word Books, 1970.

Clark, S. J. W. *The Indigenous Church*. London: World Dominion Press, 1928.

Climenhaga, A. M. "Missions and the Emerging Church." *EMQ* 1 (1965): 3–12.

Coggins, W. T. "The Risks of Sending Dollars Only." *EMQ* 24 (1988): 204–206.

————. and Frizen, E. L., Jr. eds., *Evangelical Missions Tomorrow*. (2nd ed.). South Pasedena, CA: William Carey Library, 1980.

Collins, T. "Missions and Churches in Partnership for Evangelism: A Study of the Declaration of Ibadan." *Missiology* 23, no. 3 (July 1995): 331–339.

Conlon, J. K. and Giovagnoli, M. *The Power of Two: How Companies of All Sizes Can Build Alliance Networks That Generate Business Opportunities.* San Francisco, CA: Jossey-Bass Publishers, 1998.

Conn, H. M. "The Money Barrier Between Sending and Receiving Churches." *EMQ* 14 (October 1978): 231–239.

Conway, J. *Friendship.* Grand Rapids, MI: Zondervan/Pyranee Books, 1989.

Corwin, C. and Samuel, V. "Assistance Programs Require Partnership." *EMQ* 15 (April 1979): 97–101.

Cosats, O. E. "Missions Out of Affluence." *Missiology* 1 (1973): 405–423.

————. *The Church and Its Mission: A Shattering Critique from the Third World.* Wheaton, IL: Tyndale House Publishers, 1974.

————. "Churches in Evangelistic Partnership." *The New Face of Evangelicalism: An International Symposium on the Lausanne Covenant,* pp. 143–61. Edited by C. Rene Padilla. Downers Grove, IL: InterVarsity Press, 1976.

————. "A Strategy for Third-World Missions." In D. A. Fraser (ed.), *The Church in New Frontiers for Mission.* (pp. 223–234). Monrovia, CA: MARC, 1983.

Dayton, E. R., and Fraser, D. A. *Planning Strategies for World Evangelization.* Grand Rapids, MI: Eerdmans, 1980.

DeKieffer, D. E. *The International Business Traveler's Companion.* Yarmouth, ME: Intercultural Press, 1993.

Dekker, J. and Neely, L. *The Torches of Joy,* Seattle, WA: YWAM Publishing, 1985.

DeVilbiss, F. "Filipinos and Foreigners Must Tackle the Missionary Task Together." *EMQ* 27 (1991): 372–375.

Donald, K. G. "What's Wrong with Foreign Money for National Pastors?" *EMQ* 13 (1977): 19–25.

Douglas, J. D., ed. *Let the Earth Hear His Voice: International Congress on World Evangelization*, Lausanne, Switzerland, Official Reference Volume. Minneapolis, MN.: World Wide Publications, 1975.

Downes, D. R. "The Cure for Dependency: Teach Your Churches to Give." *EMQ* 28 (1992): 142–150.

Doz, Y. L. and Hamel, G. *Alliance Advantage: The Art of Creating Value Through Partnering*. Boston, MA: Harvard Business School Press, 1998.

Engel, J. F. *A Clouded Future? Advancing North American World Missions*. Milwaukee, WI: Christian Stewardship Association, 1996.

Escobar, S. "Responses to the Article by Pate and Keyes." *IBMR* 10 (1986): 162–163.

Escobar, S. "Evangelical Missiology: Peering into the Future from a Critical Historical Moment." Paper presented at the World Evangelical Fellowship Missions Commission Missiological Consultation, Iguassu, Brazil, October, 1999.

Fernando, A. "'Rich' and 'Poor' Nations and the Christian Enterprise: Some Personal Comments." *Missiology* 9, no. 3 (July 1981): 287–298.

————. *Reclaiming Friendship*. Scottdale, PA: Herald Press, 1993.

Finley, A. and Lutz, L., *The Family Tie*. Nashville, TN: Thomas Nelson Publishers, 1983.

Flatt, D. C. "Priorities in Missions–Personnel or Programme?" *IRM* 59 (October 1970): 461–469.

Fox, F. F. "Partnership: More than a Buzzword." *EMQ* 37, no. 3 (July 2001): 294–304.

Fraser, D. A. ed. *The Church in New Frontiers for Mission.* Monrovia, CA: Missions Advanced Research and Communications Center, 1983.

Friedman, T. L. *The Lexus and the Olive Tree: Understanding Globalization.* New York, NY: Farrar, Strauss and Giroux, 1999.

Fuller, W. H. *Mission-Church Dynamics.* South Pasadena, CA: William Carey Library, 1980.

GCOWE Task Force. "Partnership Development: Partnerships Everywhere" (1995). [Online]. Available at http://www.ad2000.org/gcowe95/partners.html

Gerber, V., ed. *Missions in Creative Tension.* The Green Lake '71 Compendium. South Pasadena, CA: William Carey Library, 1971.

Glasser, A. F. ed. *Crucial Dimensions in World Evangelization.* South Pasadena, CA: William Carey Library, 1976.

Greenway, R. S. ed. *Discipling the City* (2nd ed.). Grand Rapids, MI: Baker, 1992.

————. "Eighteen Barrels and Two Big Crates." *EMQ* 28 (1992): 126–132.

Hall, E. T. *The Hidden Dimension.* Garden City, NY: Anchor Press/Doubleday, 1966.

————. *Beyond Culture.* Garden City, NY: Anchor Press/Doubleday, 1977.

————. *The Dance of Life.* Garden City, NY: Anchor Press/Doubleday, 1984.

————. and Hall, M. R. *Understanding Cultural Differences.* Yarmouth, ME: Intercultural Press, 1990.

Hamm, P. "Breaking the Power Habit: Imperatives for Multinational Mission." *EMQ* 19 (1983): 180–189.

Hanks, T. "Paternalistic—Me?" *EMQ* 8 (1972): 153–159.

Harbison, J. R. and Pekar, Jr., P. *Smart Alliances: A Practical Guide to Repeatable Success.* San Francisco, CA: Jossey-Bass Publishers, 1998.

Harris, R. M., and Patterson, Patricia J. "People in Mission: Toward Selfhood and Solidarity." *IRM* 64 (1975): 137–142.

Hedlund, R. E. "The Curses of Money on Missions to India: Two More Protests." *EMQ* 22 (1985): 297–300.

————. "Cheaper by the Dozen? Indigenous Missionaries vs. Partnership." *EMQ* 26, no. 3 (July 1990): 274–279.

————. *The Mission of the Church in the World.* Grand Rapids, MI: Baker, 1991.

Hiebert, P. G. "Critical Issues in the Social Sciences and Their Implications for Mission Studies." *Missiology* 24, no. 1 (January 1996): 77–80.

Hesselgrave, D. J. ed. *Theology and Mission.* Papers given at Trinity Consultation No. 1. Grand Rapids, MI: Baker Book House, 1978.

————. *New Horizons in World Mission: Evangelicals and the Christian Mission in the 1980s.* Papers given at Trinity Consultation No. 2. Grand Rapids, MI: Baker Book House, 1979.

————. *Today's Choices for Tomorrow's Mission.* Grand Rapids, MI: Zondervan, 1988.

"Hindrances to Cooperation: The Suspicion about Finances." *Co-operating in World Evangelization.* Lausanne Occasional Papers, 24. Wheaton, IL: Lausanne Committee for World Evangelization, 1983.

Hintze, O. C. "Complementarity: A Mature Interrelationship between Partner Churches for Better Effecting God's Mission." Th.D. dissertation, Lutheran School of Theology at Chicago, 1980.

Hodges, M. *The Indigenous Church and the Missionary.* South Pasadena, CA: William Carey Library, 1978.

Hofstede, G. *Culture's Consequences: International Differences in Work-Related Values.* Beverly Hills, CA: Sage Publications, 1984.

Hutchinson, M. and Kalu, O. eds. *A Global Faith: Essays on Evangelicalism and Globalization.* Sydney, Australia: Centre for the Study of Australian Christianity, 1998.

Jacques, E. E. "An Equal Partnership Structure." *EMQ* 9 (1973): 65–73.

Johnstone, P. *The Church Is Bigger Than You Think.* Gerrards Cross, Great Britain: WEC, 1998.

Kalu, O. U. "The Peter Pan Syndrome." *Missiology* 3 (1975): 15–29.

——————. "Not Just New Relationship but a Renewed Body." *IRM* 64 (1975): 143–147.

Kanter, R. M. *When Giants Learn to Dance.* New York, NY: Simon & Schuster, 1989.

Kato, B. "Aid to the National Church—When It Helps, When It Hinders." *EMQ* 8 (1972): 193–201.

Keener, G. H. "Critique of Internationalization of Mission." *The Seminarian* 7, no. 5 (1977): 3.

Keidel, L. "From Dependency to Dignity." *EMQ* 33 (1997): 42–47.

Kendall, G. "Missionaries Should Not Plant Churches." *EMQ* 24 (1988): 218–221.

Keyes, L. E. "The New Age of Missions: Third World Missions." In R. D. Winter and S. C. Hawthorne (Eds.), *Perspectives on the world Christian movement: A reader* (pp. 754–762). South Pasadena, CA: William Carey Library, 1981.

Keyes, L. E. "Third World Missionaries: More and Better." *EMQ* 18, no. 4 (October 1982): 216–224.

————. *The Last Age of Missions*. South Pasadena, CA: William Carey Library, 1983.

————. and Pate, Larry D. "Two-Thirds World Missions: The Next 100 Years." *Missiology* 21, no. 2 (April 1993): 187–206.

Komendant, G. and Law, G. "Western Funding for National Workers," *East-West Church and Ministry Report* 4, no. 1 (Winter 1996): 2–4.

Kornfield, W. J. "What Hath our Western Money and Our Western Gospel Wrought?" *EMQ* 27 (1991): 230–236.

Kraakevik, J. and Welliver, D., eds. *Partners in the Gospel: The Strategic Role of Partnership in World Evangelization*. Wheaton, IL: Billy Graham Center, Wheaton College, 1991.

Kraft, C. H. and Wisley, T. N. eds. *Readings in Dynamic Indigeneity*. South Pasadena, CA: William Carey Library, 1979.

Kuiper, J. M. "A Call to Die on an Old Field." *EMQ* 23 (1987): 386–392.

Latourette, K. S. *Missions Tomorrow*. New York, NY: Harper and Brothers, 1936.

Lausanne Committee for World Evangelization. *Co-operating in World Evangelization*. Lausanne Occasional Papers, no. 24. Wheaton, IL: Lausanne Committee for World Evangelization, 1983.

Lausanne Committee for World Evangelization. *The Manila Manifesto: an Elaboration of the Lausanne Covenant, Fifteen Years Later*. Pasadena, CA: Lausanne Committee for World Evangelization, 1989.

Lee, E. M. "West and East Must Get Along—A Korean Missionary Speaks Out." *EMQ* 19 (1983): 190–195.

Lewis, J. D. *Partnerships for Profit: Structuring and Managing Strategic Alliances.* New York, NY: The Free Press, 1990.

Linnartz, H. C. "Asian Christians Embrace Responsibility, Shun Paternalism at Missions Congress." *Pulse* 25 (October 12, 1990): 4.

Lipnack, J. and Stamps, J. *The Age of The Network: Organizing Principles for the 21st Century.* Essex Junction, VT: Oliver Wight Publications, 1994.

Lodge, G. C. *Managing Globalization in the Age of Interdependence.* San Diego, CA: Pfeiffer & Company, 1995.

Lundy, J. D., *We Are the World: Globalization and the Changing Face of Missions.* Cumbrian, UK: O. M. Publishing, 1999.

Marshall, P. with Gilbert, L. *Their Blood Cries Out: The Untold Story of Persecution Against Christians in the Modern World.* Dallas, TX: Word Publishing, 1997.

McGavran, D. A.; Montgomery, J.; and Wagner, C. P. "Thrashing Old Straw." *Church Growth Bulletin* (1980): 306–311.

McGinnis, A. L. *The Friendship Factor.* Minneapolis, MN: Augsburg Publishing House, 1979.

McQuilkin, R. "Six Inflammatory Questions." *EMQ* 30 (1994): 130–134.

Mott, John R. *Cooperation and the World Mission.* New York, NY: International Missionary Council, 1935.

Mumper, S. "An Indonesian Leader Speaks to the West: An Interview with Chris Marantika." *EMQ* 22 (1986): 6–11.

Neill, S. *Christian Partnership.* London: SCM Press, 1952.

————. *Creative Tension: The Duff Lectures, 1958.* London: Edinburgh House Press, 1959.

Nelson, M. L. *Readings in Third World Missions: A Collection of Essential Documents*. South Pasadena, CA: William Carey Library, 1976.

———— *The How and Why of Third World Missions: An Asian Case Study*. South Pasadena, CA: William Carey Library, 1976.

Nevius, J. *Planting and Development of Missionary Churches*, rev., ed., Phillipsburg, PA: Presbyterian and Reformed Publishing House, 1958.

Newbigin, L. *One Body, One Gospel, One World: The Christian Mission Today*. London: n. p., 1959.

Niringiye, D. Z. "Africans in Missions: The Possible Dream." *EMQ* 31 (1995): 54–60.

O'Hara-Devereaux, M. and Johansen, R. *Globalwork: Bridging Distance, Culture and Time*. San Francisco, CA: Jossey-Bass Publishers, 1994.

Ott, C. "Let the Buyer Beware." *EMQ* 29 (1993): 286–291.

Padilla, C. R. ed. *The New Face of Evangelicalism*. Downers Grove, IL: Inter Varsity Press, 1976.

Pate, L. D. "Get Ready for Partnerships with Emerging Missions." *EMQ* 22 (1986): 382–388.

———— and Keyes, L. E. "Emerging Missions in a Global Church." *International Bulletin of Missionary Research* 10, no. 4 (October 1986): 156–165.

Pate, L. D. *From Every People: a Handbook of Two-Thirds World Missions with Directory/Histories/Analysis*. Monrovia, CA: MARC, 1989.

———— "The Changing Balance in Global Mission." *IBMR* 15, no. 2 (April 1991): 56–61.

Pentecost, E. C. "A New Emphasis on Partnership." *EMQ* 22 (1986): 314–315.

Peters, G. W. *A Biblical Theology of Missions*. Chicago, IL: Moody Press, 1972.

———— "Mission-Church Relationships," I and II. *Bibliotheca Sacra* 125 (499): 205–215 (500): 300–312.

———— "Pauline Patterns of Church-Mission Relationships." *EMQ* 9 (Winter 1973): 111–118.

Rackham, N., Friedman, L. and Ruff, R. *Getting Partnering Right: How Market Leaders Are Creating Long-Term Competitive Advantage*. New York, NY: McGraw Hill, 1996.

Reapsome, J. "Our Generosity: Is It Really Helping?" *EMQ* 18 (1982): 190–192.

———— "AIM Sends First Missionary from Brazil to Mozambique." *Pulse* 26 (April 26, 1991): 2.

———— "Partnerships Are Crucial to Success of Missions, Consultation Declares." *Pulse* 28 (June 28: 1991): 5.

Reed, N. E. "Five Principles of Indigenous Church Organizations: Lessons from a Brazilian Pentecostal Church." *Missiology: An International Review* 17 (January, 1989): 39–51.

Reichenbach, B. R. "The Captivity of Third World Churches." *EMQ* 18 (1982): 166–179.

Rickett, D. and Welliver, D., eds. *Supporting Indigenous Ministries: With Selected Readings*. Wheaton, IL: Billy Graham Center, Wheaton College, 1997.

Rickett, D. "Preventing Dependency: Developmental Partnering." *EMQ* 34, no. 4 (October 1998): 438–445.

————. *Building Strategic Relationships: A Practical Guide to Partnering with Non-Western Missions*. San Jose, CA: Partners International, 2000.

————. "Seven Mistakes Partners Make and How to Avoid Them."
EMQ 37 (July 2001): 308–317.

Robert, D. L. "Shifting Southward: Global Christianity Since 1945."
IBMR (April 2000): 50–57.

Samuel, V., and Sugden, C. "The Two-Thirds World Church and the
Multinational Mission Agencies." *Missiology* 10, no. 4 (October
1982): 449–454.

————. and Sugden, C. "Mission Agencies as Multinationals." *IBMR*
17 (October 1983): 152–155.

Sawatsky, W. "After the Glasnost Revolution: Soviet Evangelicals and
Western Missions." *IBMR* 16, no. 2 (April 1992): 54–60.

Scherer, J. A. *Missionary Go Home: A Reappraisal of the Christian World
Mission.* Englewood Cliffs, NJ: Prentice-Hall, 1964.

Schipper, G. J. "Non-Western Missionaries: Our Newest Challenge."
EMQ 24 (1988): 198–202.

Schwartz, G. J. "From Dependency to Fulfillment." *EMQ* 27 (1991):
238–241.

————. "It's Time to Get Serious about the Cycle of Dependency in
Africa." *EMQ* 29 (1993): 126–130.

————. "Cutting the Apron Strings." *EMQ* 30 (1994): 36–43.

Senge, P. M., Kleiner, A., Roberts, C., Ross, R. B., and Smith, B. J. *The
Fifth Discipline Fieldbook: Strategies and Tools for Building a Learning Organization.* New York, NY: Doubleday/Currency, 1994.

Shaw, R. B. *Trust in the Balance: Building Successful Organizations on
Results, Integrity, and Concern.* San Francisco, CA: Jossey-Bass
Publishers, 1997.

Shenk, C. E. "Internationalization of Mission." *The Seminarian* 7, no.
5 (1977): 1–3.

Shenk, W. R. ed. *Mission Focus: Current Issues*. Scottdale, PA: Herald Press, 1980.

—————. "Toward a Global Church History." *IBMR* 20 (1996): 50–57.

Shorb, T. B. "Third-Era Missionary Partnerships between Western Agencies and Agencies from the Two-Thirds World." Ph.D. dissertation, Trinity Theological Seminary, Newburgh, Indiana, 1997.

Sims, R. J. "Wealth and Poverty, Self-Support and Sharing in the Church Worldwide: A Biblical Study with Missiological Implication." M.A. thesis, Fuller Theological Seminary, 1989.

Sine, T. ed. *The Church in Response to Human Need*. Monrovia, CA: Missions Advanced Research and Communication Center, 1983.

Skreslet, S. H. "The Empty Basket of Presbyterian Mission: Limits and Possibilities of Partnership." *IBMR* 19 (1995): 98–104.

Smith, D. K. *Creating Understanding*. Grand Rapids, MI: Zondervan Publishing House, 1992.

Smith, D. P. "Slaying the Dragons of Self-interest: Making International Partnership Work." *EMQ* 28 (1992): 18–23.

Smith, H. "Ministry in Cuba: The Right Questions to Ask." *EMQ* 33 (1997): 60–67.

Smith, Robert [pseud.]. "The Use of Foreign Financed National Christian Workers." *International Journal of Frontier Missions* 9, no. 2 (April 1992): 57–63.

Sookhdeo, P. ed. *New Frontiers in Mission*. Exeter, UK: Paternoster, 1987.

—————. "Cultural Issues in Partnership in Mission." In Taylor, W. D., ed., *Kingdom Partnerships for Synergy in Missions*. South Pasadena, CA: William Carey Library, 1994.

Stanley, R.; Hedlund, R.; and Masih, J. P. "The Curses of Money on Missions to India." *EMQ* 22, no. 3 (July 1986): 294–302.

Stott, J. *The Lausanne Covenant: An Exposition and Commentary*. Minneapolis, MN: World Wide Publications, 1975.

Strong, R. "Practical Partnership with Churches Overseas." *IRM* 61 (1972): 281–287.

Taber, C. R. "Money, Power and Mission." *The Other Side* (March–April 1976): 28–34, 43–44.

———. "Structures and Strategies for Interdependence in World Mission." In Shenk, W. R., ed., *Mission Focus: Current Issues*. Scottdale, PA: Herald Press, 1980.

Taylor, W. D. ed. *Internationalising Missionary Training: A Global Perspective*. Exeter, UK: Paternoster, 1991.

———. ed. *Kingdom Partnerships for Synergy in Missions*. South Pasadena, CA: William Carey Library, World Evangelical Fellowship Missions Commission, 1994.

———. "Lessons of Partnership." *EMQ* 31, no. 4 (October 1995): 406–415.

Toews, J. E. "Biblical Foundations for Interdependence." In *Mission Focus: Current Issues*, pp. 129–36. Edited by Wilbert R. Shenk. Scottdale, PA: Herald Press, 1980.

Trompenaars, F. *Riding the Waves of Culture: Understanding Diversity in Global Business*. Chicago, IL: IRWIN, 1994.

Vikner, D. L. "The era of Interdependence." *Missiology* 2 (1974): 475–488.

Ward, T. "Christian Missions: Survival in What Form?" *IBM,* 6 (January 1982): 2–3.

Wagner, C. P. ed. *Church/Mission Tensions Today*. Chicago, IL: Moody Press, 1972.

Wakatama, P. *Independence for the Third World Church.* Downers Grove, IL: Inter Varsity Press, 1976.

————. "The Role of Africans in the World Mission of the Church." *EMQ* 26 (1990): 126–130.

Walls, A. *The Missionary Movement in Christian History.* Maryknoll: Orbis, 1996.

Walz, B. "The Hard Road to Missions Vision in National Churches." *EMQ* 30 (1994): 414–422.

Warren, M., ed. *To Apply the Gospel, Selections from the Writings of Henry Venn.* Grand Rapids, MI: Eerdmans, 1970.

Williams, T. "Indian Missionaries: How Should They Be Used?" *EMQ* 16 (1980): 221–224.

————. ed. *World Missions: Building Bridges or Barriers?* (2nd ed.). Bangalore, India: World Evangelical Fellowship Missions Commission, 1980.

Winer, M. and Ray, K. *Collaboration Handbook: Creating, Sustaining, and Enjoying the Journey.* Saint Paul, MN: Amherst H. Wilder Foundation, 1994.

Winter, R. D. "The Concept of a Third Era in Missions." *EMQ* 17 (1981): 69–82.

————. and Hawthorne, H. C. eds. *Perspectives on the World Christian Movement: A Reader.* South Pasadena, CA: William Carey Library, 1981.

Winter, R. D. "Why Sending Money Does Not Work as Well as Sending People." *Missions Frontiers* 16 (September/October, 1994): 12–13.

Yohannan, K. P. *Why the World Waits.* Lake Mary, FL: Creation House, 1991.

Partners International

Partners International is a global ministry that works to create and grow communities of Christian witness in partnership with God's people in the least Christian regions of the world.

Since 1943, Partners International has initiated strategic partnerships with effective indigenous ministries that focus on starting churches where none exist. Working in the least economically developed countries and in areas restricted to Christian witness, our key approach is holistic witness (word and deed)—to alleviate human suffering and share the gospel.

For more information, please visit

www.partnersintl.org

or write to:

Partners International
1313 N. Atlantic Street, Suite 4000
Spokane, WA 99201.

(509) 343-4000
(800) 966-5515
Fax (509) 343-4015

To order additional copies of

MAKING YOUR PARTNERSHIP WORK

Have your credit card ready and call

Toll free: (877) 421-READ (7323)

or send $14.95 each plus $4.95 S&H* to

WinePress Publishing
PO Box 428
Enumclaw, WA 98022

www.winepresspub.com

*WA residents, add 8.6% sales tax

*add $1.00 S&H for each additional book ordered